THE HISTORY OF ARMIES AROUND THE WORLD

THE HISTORY OF
ARMIES
AROUND THE WORLD

EDITED BY SHALINI SAXENA
SUPPLEMENTAL MATERIAL BY MICHAEL RAY

Britannica®
Educational Publishing
IN ASSOCIATION WITH

ROSEN
EDUCATIONAL SERVICES

Published in 2014 by Britannica Educational Publishing (a trademark of Encyclopædia Britannica, Inc.) in association with The Rosen Publishing Group, Inc.
29 East 21st Street, New York, NY 10010

Distributed exclusively by Rosen Publishing.
To see additional Britannica Educational Publishing titles, go to rosenpublishing.com

First Edition

Britannica Educational Publishing
J.E. Luebering: Director, Core Reference Group
Anthony L. Green: Editor, Compton's by Britannica

Rosen Publishing
Hope Lourie Killcoyne: Executive Editor
Shalini Saxena: Editor
Nelson Sá: Art Director
Nelson Sá: Designer
Cindy Reiman: Photography Manager
Introduction by Shalini Saxena

Cataloging-in-Publication Data

Saxena, Shalini.
The history of armies around the world/Shalini Saxena; supplementary material by Michael Ray.—First edition.
        pages cm.—(The world's armed forces)
"In association with Britannica Educational Publishing, Rosen Educational Services."
Includes bibliographical references and index.
ISBN 978-1-62275-139-6 (library binding)
1. Armies—History. 2. Military history. I. Title.
UA15.S29 2014
355.009—dc23
                                                                    2013022938

Manufactured in the United States of America.

On the cover, p. 3: (Top) Paratroopers of the British Army conducting strike operations in Afghanistan. *Marco Di Lauro/Getty Images.* (Bottom left) Special forces of the Iranian Army marching during a parade in Tehran. *Behrouz Mehri/AFP/Getty Images.* (Bottom right) Recruits of the People's Liberation Army of China marching. *TPG/Getty Images.*

CONTENTS

Ancient Greek armor from Magna Graecia exhibited at the Metropolitan Museum of Art. A bronze helmet, cuirass (body armor), and two bronze shin guards can be seen on display along-side horse armor. Universal Images Group/Getty Images

Armies—large organized forces armed and trained for war, especially on land—have existed in one form or another for millennia. Armies have been made up of professionals or amateurs, of mercenaries fighting for pay or for plunder, or of patriots fighting for a cause. Today, most countries have a standing army that is often the largest and oldest branch of the military. The following pages chronicle the development of armies around the world, examining how they have become the formidable forces they are today.

At various times armies have been built around infantry soldiers or mounted warriors or men in machines. More than 5,000 years ago, in the wars between civilizations of the Middle East, foot soldiers were the main combatants. This changed during the Middle Ages when soldiers were mainly mounted warriors. Nearly all the great armies of the period were dominated by cavalry, including the Christian knights of Europe, the armies of Islam, and the hordes of Mongol warriors from East Asia.

The resurgence of the foot soldier came with the introduction of gunpowder into warfare, one of the most decisive changes to warfare and to the organization of armies. The difference gunpowder made may be best summed up in the word "distance." Prior to the appearance of gunpowder, land battles were mostly hand-to-hand combat. Whether soldiers were on foot, on horseback, or in chariots, the weapons were much the same, and battles were fought as close encounters. Gunpowder made it possible to kill an enemy hundreds of feet away.

Bombs, a natural outgrowth of gunpowder, and nuclear weapons also revolutionized warfare, changing the nature of many army operations. While foot soldiers are still the main combatants in most wars, modern infantrymen are supported by aircraft, artillery, tanks, and all the complexities of modern communication systems. Modern warfare—with its land, air, and sea components—has greatly enlarged the field of operations beyond a single battlefield, as evident in the wars of the 21st century.

As militaries have become more inclusive of women and gays in service, armies have become increasingly diverse in composition. New weapons and technologies have revolutionized battle tactics and the nature of war. Yet even as military policies, technologies, weapons, and strategies continue to evolve, armies remain an enduring and crucial part of armed forces around the world.

WHAT IS AN ARMY?

CHAPTER 1

An army is an organized, land-based military fighting unit. From the ancient world to modern times, the organization and composition of armies has varied considerably.

COMPOSITION OF ARMIES

The earliest armies consisted of warriors in horse-drawn chariots; infantry—armed foot soldiers; and cavalry—armed soldiers on horseback. These units were sometimes accompanied by engineers who operated siege weapons and by supply trains to feed and outfit the fighters.

With the introduction of cannon in the 15th century, artillery units were added to the combat sections of armies. In the 19th and 20th centuries, as a result of great advances in technology, other units were added: signal troops, engineer corps for

A 15th-century cannon. Ingvar Tjostheim/Shutterstock.com

building bridges and entrenchments, medical units, administrative troops, mechanized units to replace cavalry, transportation and communication units, and explosives and munitions experts. The number of such backup or support units has tended to increase as warfare has become more sophisticated.

CONSCRIPTION

Conscription is the compulsory enrollment for service in a country's armed forces. It has existed at least since the Egyptian Old Kingdom in the 27th century BCE. It usually takes the form of selective service rather than universal conscription. (The latter generally refers to compulsory military service by all able-bodied men between certain ages, though a few countries—notably Israel—have also drafted women.) In the 19th century Prussia's system of building up a large standing army through conscription became the model for competing European powers. During the American Civil War both the federal government and the Confederacy instituted a draft, but the U.S. did not use it again until entering World War I in 1917. Like the U.S., Britain abandoned conscription at the end of World War I but reverted to it when World War II threatened. Britain retained the draft until 1960. In the United States, although peacetime conscription on a selective basis was ended in 1973 as part of a program to establish an all-volunteer military service, registration for a future draft if needed was reinstituted in 1980.

Recruitment for armies takes different forms. Soldiers may be volunteers, conscripts, or mercenaries. Volunteers fight willingly, usually for a cause or a country. Conscripts are drafted by their country to serve in its armed forces. Mercenaries serve for pay. They are not necessarily citizens of the country they fight for.

COMMAND STRUCTURES

The command structure of armies has undergone considerable change in the course of centuries. The earliest armies followed a single leader, either a tribal chief or a king. As nations grew in size and armies became larger, it was necessary to divide command among officers, of whom generals were the highest rank. Officers, some of whom were professional soldiers, normally came from the wealthiest class in a society. They alone had the money to pay soldiers, buy weapons, and supply horses for war.

In the 21st century, with the spread of both democratic and socialist types of government, permanent officer classes based on wealth or heredity have tended to disappear. Except in states that have military dictatorships, the army is kept under the control of elected civilian officials. Officers are promoted from within the ranks or are trained at military schools.

Command structures of modern armies vary somewhat. The officer ranking system discussed here is based on that of the United States Army as it has developed since World War II.

All army personnel are ranked according to level, from the lowest level—privates—to the highest level—generals. Above privates there are three levels of officers: noncommissioned officers, warrant officers, and commissioned officers. The difference between noncommissioned officers and commissioned officers is one of training and also of authority. Commissioned officers are graduates of military academies or of officer training schools. Additionally, those trained in certain professional fields may be directly commissioned as officers to serve in the Army Medical Department, the Army Judge Advocate General Corps, or the Army Chaplain Corps.

Noncommissioned officers include corporals and sergeants. There are several ranks of sergeants including staff sergeant, master sergeant, and command sergeant major. The

UNITED STATES MILITARY ACADEMY

Founded in 1802 at the fort at West Point, N.Y., the United States Military Academy is one of the oldest service academies in the world. It was established as an apprentice school for military engineers and was, in effect, the first U.S. school of engineering. It was reorganized in 1812, and in 1866 its educational program was expanded considerably. Women were first admitted in 1976. The four-year course of college-level education and training leads to a bachelor of science degree and a commission as second lieutenant in the Army.

Color guard of the U.S. Military Academy, West Point, New York, during morning exercises. U.S. Army Photo

Cadets must be at least 17 years of age but not yet 23. They must be unmarried and not pregnant, as well as not legally responsible for the support of a child at the time of their appointment. They must have a high-school education or its equivalent and must take scholastic-aptitude tests and a medical examination before admission. Enrollment in a typical year is over 4,000. The great majority of appointments to the academy are made by U.S. senators and representatives. Citizens of more than 150 other countries, if fully qualified, may also be admitted to the academy, although the total enrollment of international cadets is capped at 60.

The academic year lasts from August to May, inclusive. The third class (sophomores) receives extensive field training at the training areas on the academy reservation. The second and first classes (juniors and seniors) obtain supplementary instruction at other Army training centers. The second class also takes part in joint amphibious maneuvers with the midshipmen from the United States Naval Academy, Annapolis, Md. First classmen serve as instructors for the new fourth class (freshmen), which enters the academy in July; they also assist in training the third class.

West Point has trained such leaders as Ulysses S. Grant, William T. Sherman, Robert E. Lee, Stonewall Jackson, Jefferson Davis, John Pershing, Dwight D. Eisenhower, Douglas MacArthur, Omar Bradley, George Patton, H. Norman Schwarzkopf, David Petraeus, and Stanley McChrystal.

duties of these officers vary considerably, depending on the complexity of the makeup of an army. Some are in combat command positions, others in backup units such as maintenance, transportation, or communications. Noncommissioned officers are promoted from within the body of enlisted personnel.

Warrant officers are neither commissioned nor noncommissioned officers, but in rank they are between the two. In the modern army, warrant officers are highly trained technical experts who usually operate in one area of specialization throughout their whole military career. Most helicopter pilots, for instance, are warrant officers. They may also operate in an advisory or administrative position, but they do not command troops. Although they remain warrant officers, their pay schedules may rise to that of some commissioned officers.

The levels of commissioned officers are as follows:

1. Line officers, also called company grade officers or junior officers, include second lieutenants, lieutenants, and captains. The highest rank, the captain, is usually in command of a company, a

A chief warrant officer of the United States Army accompanies an Iraqi pilot as he tests a helicopter during a training period in Iraq. DVIDS/ Spc. Amie McMillan

unit of approximately 100-200 soldiers in the United States Army. A lieutenant commands a platoon, a unit of approximately 20 to 40 soldiers. He is assisted by a second lieutenant. The promotion path from second lieutenant to captain generally takes about four years; directly commissioned officers are

THE HISTORY OF ARMIES AROUND THE WORLD

an exception to this, as most are promoted to captain within their first year of service.

2. Field grade officers, also called senior officers, are majors, lieutenant colonels, and colonels. Colonels command brigades, units of 3,000 to 5,000 soldiers. Lieutenant colonels command battalions, units of approximately 600 soldiers. They are assisted by majors.

3. General officers are the highest ranking officers in an army. They are brigadier general, major general, lieutenant general, and general. Some European armies have as the highest rank the field marshal. The United States has conferred the unique title of general of the armies on a few generals of notable achievement such as John J. Pershing, George C. Marshall, Dwight D. Eisenhower, Douglas MacArthur, Omar Bradley, and Henry H. Arnold. This title is the equivalent of the European field marshal. In terms of rank, major generals are in charge of divisions (10,000 to 18,000 soldiers); lieutenant generals command an army corps (two or more divisions);

and generals command a field army (100,000 or more soldiers). The army units named here are based on the modern United States Army and do not coincide exactly with those of other major armies of the world.

In most modern armies the distinction is made between line officers and staff officers. Line officers are those in charge of the purely combatant section of an army. Staff officers are general officers who assist the commander of a military force. The United

General Dwight D. Eisenhower speaks with a soldier in England in 1944. He was honored with the title General of the Army the same year. **Popperfoto/Getty Images**

States, for instance, has a Department of the Army responsible to the president as commander in chief. The staff officers plan and coordinate the activities of an army in both peace and war.

The first such officer staff was the General Staff established in Prussia in 1806 by Gen. Gerhard von Scharnhorst. With the unification of Germany in 1871 it became the German General Staff, a highly effective model for all other command systems. By the start of World War I all major armies of the world had command staffs.

Since World War II the staffs of the separate military branches—army, navy, and air force—have been combined into a joint staff arrangement. The United States has a Joint Chiefs of Staff responsible to the secretary of defense and to the president. Other major military powers such as Great Britain, France, and Israel have similar military command structures.

ANCIENT ARMIES

The first historical evidence of army organization comes from the Middle Eastern Sumerian empire in Babylonia. Figurines from the 4th millennium BCE show foot soldiers in copper helmets and heavy cloaks carrying short spears. The Sumerians used wooden chariots; but, with four solid wooden wheels, these were probably too slow to ride into battle.

The army of the Babylonians (2nd millennium BCE) included both lifetime soldiers drawn from the highest social class and citizens from the merchant class. The lifetime soldiers received grants of land for their service. They could pass the land on to their sons only if the sons, too, became soldiers. The conscripts may have been rewarded for their service with special trading or fishing privileges.

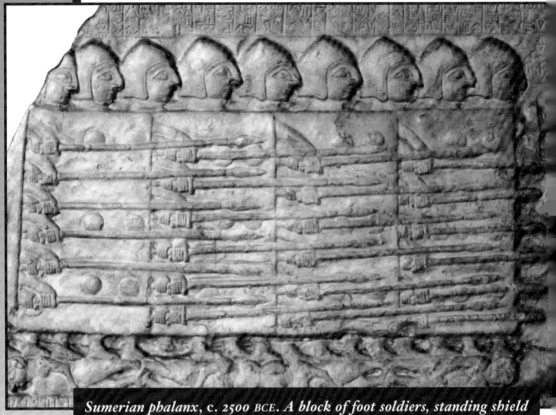

Sumerian phalanx, c. 2500 BCE. A block of foot soldiers, standing shield to shield and presenting spears, advances in a dense mass typical of the phalanx. From the Stele of the Vultures, limestone bas-relief, c. 2500 BCE. In the Louvre, Paris. Giraudon/Art Resource, New York

ANCIENT EGYPT

The Egyptians of the New Kingdom (1560–1085 BCE) built up their army in two ways: by recruiting citizens and by enlisting foreign troops. Some of the foreign troops were slaves from conquered lands. In this way Egypt shifted to her subject nations the burden of

A relief of Ramses II defeating his enemies. Kenneth Garrett/National Geographic Image Collection/Getty Images

supplying fighting men. Other foreign fighters were mercenaries paid in land or plunder. The resulting settlements of Nubian, Libyan, and Greek mercenaries in Egypt became so powerful that it was difficult for later pharaohs, or kings, to rule them. From about 945 to 730 BCE Egypt was ruled by descendants of Libyan settlers.

The army of Egypt's New Kingdom was divided into infantry and chariot forces. Each light, two-wheeled chariot carried a driver and an archer. Foot soldiers fought with copper or bronze axes, daggers, scimitars, and bows and arrows. In 1320 BCE the standing army consisted of two divisions of 2,000 men each. Each division had eight companies of 250 archers and spearmen. Each company had five platoons of 50 men. These soldiers wore helmets and either leather breastplates covered with metal scales or cloth tunics covered with crocodile skin.

Egypt's army was probably strongest under the warlike pharaoh Ramses II (reigned 1304–1237 BCE), who commanded four Egyptian infantry divisions, bands of Nubian archers, and many other mercenaries—a total of 20,000 men.

Assyria

Four centuries after Ramses' reign, an Assyrian king, Shalmaneser II, boasted that he could raise an army of 120,000 men. The core of the Assyrian army was the king's bodyguard, a group of highly trained professional soldiers. Every Assyrian landowner could also be drafted. Assyrian sculptures show the king riding out to battle in a chariot surrounded by the Royal Guard. The richest men could afford to have chariots, horses, and attendants. Chariots probably led the attack. The riders had to fire arrows while driving at a gallop.

The Assyrians had the first known cavalry, a force of men on horseback. These men wore coats of iron scales and leather breeches. They either thrust at the enemy with nine-foot (2.7-meter) spears or shot arrows. Most Assyrian soldiers fought on foot. The foot soldiers were divided into heavily armed troops with pointed helmets, coats of mail (linked metal armor), and metal or wicker shields, and lightly armed troops with helmets and wicker shields. Slingers hurled stones at the enemy with slingshots. Other groups carried six-foot

(1.8-m) spears and straight swords made of bronze or iron. The favorite weapon of the Assyrians seems to have been the bow and arrow. Baggage animals and herds of animals to feed the army followed behind the soldiers.

ANCIENT GREECE

While Assyria was a unified empire, Greece was made up of independent city-states, each with its own army. At first the armies were small and made up of free men. Slaves were not used as soldiers because defending the city was considered an honor. All men served as border guards from age 18 to 20. During this time, they learned how to use shield, spear, and sword and to fight in a formation called a phalanx.

A phalanx consisted of eight or more lines of infantry, one behind the other, drawn up across a battlefield. The men stood shoulder to shoulder, and each successive line followed the one in front of it closely. An individual soldier was called a hoplite, from the Greek word for heavy infantry. The lines moved forward at the same time, making a charge a heavy shock to the enemy. As men in the front line fell, those in the next line moved forward to replace them in combat. Fighting in this

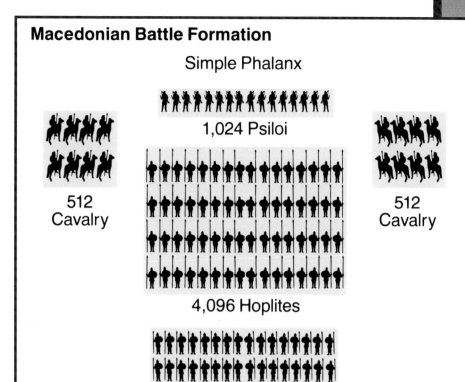

Macedonian Battle Formation

Simple Phalanx

1,024 Psiloi

512 Cavalry

512 Cavalry

4,096 Hoplites

2,048 Peltasts

The battle formation developed by Macedonian king Philip II and his son, Alexander the Great, improved the phalanx. **Encyclopædia Britannica, Inc.**

manner did not require much training, but Greek soldiers in Athens and most city-states did not remain in the army very long. After age 20 they fought only when called upon. Each soldier supported himself and bought his own weapons and supplies. Command of the army did not belong to a king or to one powerful general. Instead, a group of men often commanded together. At the battle of Marathon, in 490 BCE, Athens had 11 generals

PHILIP II

Ancient Macedonia grew into a powerful and united country under the leadership of Philip II, or Philip of Macedon (382–336 BCE). By 338 BCE, through warfare and diplomacy, Philip established Macedonian rule over all of Greece. His conquests laid the foundation for the mighty empire built by his son, Alexander the Great.

Philip, a son of King Amyntas III, was born in 382 BCE. In his boyhood he saw the Macedonian kingdom falter because of internal strife and interference by neighboring powers. Philip spent some time as a hostage in the strong Greek city of Thebes. There he learned about military tactics by observing the great Greek general Epaminondas.

Philip came to the throne suddenly in 359, when his brother was killed during an invasion by the Illyrians. At first Philip promoted peace with his neighbors. Meanwhile, he built up his army and introduced innovations in arms, tactics, and training.

Macedonia's expansion began with victories over the Illyrians and other northern enemies. On the eastern frontier, Philip's movements provoked the Greeks into forming a coalition against him, but it could not stop his conquests. Philip also assisted Thebes and the Thessalian League of city-states in a war against the Phocians. After a spectacular victory in Thessaly, he was elected president of the Thessalian League.

Philip's growing influence alarmed the great orator Demosthenes at Athens. He spoke tirelessly of the threat that he believed Philip posed to Greek freedom.

Demosthenes' speeches turned Athens against Philip, and Thebes also came to view him as a threat. In 338 Philip, with help from Alexander, defeated both Athens and Thebes at the battle of Chaeronea. The victory made Philip the leader of Greece.

Philip then set his sights on Persia. In preparation for an attack, he organized all the Greek states except Sparta into an alliance called the League of Corinth. Before Philip could carry out his plan, however, he was undone by family politics. After he took a second wife, his first wife, Olympias, left him, taking Alexander. In 336 Philip was assassinated by a Macedonian nobleman, possibly in collusion with Olympias and Alexander.

who voted on strategy. Every day a different one of the 11 took charge.

In Sparta, the most militaristic Greek city-state, all free male citizens were full-time soldiers. They began training at age seven. At 20, each man joined a company made up of 15 men. Each member of the group had to help pay for the food. The men in the company ate, trained and fought together. Even if they had families, the soldiers lived with their company in a military camp until age 30. Because the soldiers did no other kind of work, the state gave each one some land and slaves to support himself and his family. The Spartans had two kings, one of whom led the army.

As the Greek city-states expanded, they had to modify the way they fought. The phalanx was not very flexible. Once it started moving, it was hard to change its direction. An opponent with cavalry or lighter troops could outflank the phalanx and attack it on the sides. To protect their flanks, the Greeks hired professional skirmishers or peltasts. The peltasts carried small round shields, swords, and javelins. They did not fight in formation but moved forward and back with the flow of battle. Gradually the Greek armies became paid professional forces.

Philip II of Macedon did a major army reorganization and created one of the most effective land-based fighting units in history. He changed the structure of the phalanx by making it 16 lines deep instead of eight. A single division of hoplites numbered 4,096 — 16 lines of 256 soldiers each. Preceding the hoplites into battle were four lines of 256 *psiloi*, light infantry. Behind the phalanx division were eight lines of 256 peltasts, also light infantry. Cavalry units covered the flanks. Including cavalry, a full division consisted of 8,192 men. Attached to the army were a medical corps and a corps of engineers. This army was inherited by Philip's son, Alexander the Great, and used to conquer a great portion of the Mediterranean world.

CARTHAGE AND ANCIENT ROME

In the western Mediterranean, somewhat removed from the activities of Greece and Macedon, two other military powers emerged: Carthage and Rome. Both began as city-states and both enlarged themselves into empires. Carthage in North Africa and Rome on the Italian peninsula were close enough to come into conflict over the control of the Mediterranean and adjacent lands. Between 264 and 146 BCE they fought three wars that resulted in final victory for Rome.

The army of Carthage, based on the early Greek phalanx, was comprised of mercenaries, yet it had the distinction of nearly annihilating the Roman army during the Second Punic War (218-201 BCE). The great Carthaginian general Hannibal was, like Napoleon 2,000 years later, a master strategist who had the ability to select the most favorable terrain for a battle. His successful tactic at the battle of Cannae in 216 BCE was to allow his light infantry to fall back before the Roman advance. The Carthaginian cavalry then moved out to the flanks to surround the numerically superior Roman army.

This victory was not followed up for several reasons: Hannibal's lack of naval support, his very long supply lines, and inadequate recruitment policies to obtain more mercenaries. The war ended eventually in a Roman victory. In the Third Punic War from 149 to 146 BCE Rome destroyed the city of Carthage and annexed the region as a Roman province.

The history of Rome is basically the history of its highly successful armies. Between the 2nd century BCE and the 1st century CE Rome expanded from a city-state to an empire controlling the whole Mediterranean basin. This achievement was the work of its legions.

The earliest Roman army formation was the phalanx, the formation used by the Greeks, Macedonians, and Carthaginians. For the Romans the phalanx proved to be too unwieldy a unit to fight on hilly and broken ground, and they soon began to change the nature of their battle formations. The result was the legion. Unlike the phalanx, the legion was not a static form; it varied greatly over the centuries.

Roman Legion Formations

Early Legion (c. 220 B.C.)

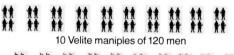

10 Velite maniples of 120 men

10 Hastati maniples of 120 men

10 Principe maniples of 120 men

10 Triarii maniples of 60 men

Marian Legion (c. 110 B.C.)

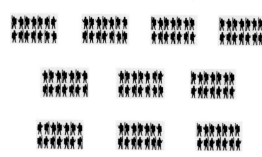

10 Cohorts of 400 men

The small fighting units of the Romans were more flexible in battle than was the Greek phalanx. **Encyclopædia Britannica, Inc.**

The term "legion" did not originally mean any specific type of military formation. Its origin probably denoted those who were chosen for military service during the annual public assembly of citizens. As it developed, the legion became a unit of from 4,000 to 6,000 heavy infantry supported by cavalry and light infantry. The term "infantry" simply means soldiers who fight on foot; the terms "light" and "heavy" refer to the kinds and weight of their weapons.

The advantage the legion had over the phalanx was flexibility and mobility. The legion did not have to move in a solid block of men as did the phalanx. The legion was divided into maniples, groups of 120 men, which were able to fight in a much more open and versatile battle array; they marched in lines instead of solid formation.

On the march soldiers carried weapons, armor, cooking gear, and tools. Each day the army would stop and build a camp surrounded by a wall of logs and a deep ditch. With the army went a train of baggage animals, armorers, supply staff, engineers, and secretaries.

From the earliest days of the Republic until the end of the 2nd century BCE the armies of Rome were made up of citizens called up for duty each year. Every male citizen between the ages of 17 and 46 was liable for duty. In times of extreme emergency all male citizens could be called up, even the young and the aged. Each class of citizens had to furnish a specific number of companies made up of 100 men. These units were called centuries, or hundreds, and they were commanded by officers called centurions. Even after the units of one hundred were abandoned, the term "centurion" persisted as an officer designation.

Shortly before the end of the 2nd century BCE a number of changes were made in the Roman army system that were to change the very nature of Rome itself. Reliance on an annual call-up of citizens meant that

Rome never had a permanent army. This practice was abandoned. The citizen army was replaced by a standing army made up of landless city dwellers and newly created citizens from outlying provinces. The allegiance of these new legions was to their commander rather than to the Roman state. The commander was expected to pay his soldiers in money or land supplied by the state.

The leader in this reform of Rome's military system was the general Gaius Marius. He reformed the legion, substituting for the maniple a 600-man unit that was called the cohort. The soldiers swore an oath to him, binding them to service for a period of ten years. This transformation from a temporary citizen army to a professional one made better training possible. It also meant that each Roman commander had his own private army, with legions that were faithful to him for their term of service.

This new army system paved the way for the destruction of the Roman Republic and the establishing of the empire. Army commanders not only went abroad making new conquests and fighting barbarians, but also vied with each other for political control of the Republic. During the 1st century BCE, Roman legions often fought each other under the leadership of such generals as Pompey, Julius Caesar, Mark Antony, and Octavian.

In the end, it was Octavian, later called Augustus Caesar, who defeated all his opponents and instituted imperial rule at Rome. Once in power, he revised the army system by cutting the number of legions from 60 to 28, requiring 20 years of service from the soldiers, and setting up a military treasury to pay the armies in the field and in retirement.

Under the empire the main task of the legions was not conquest, but defense. The extensive borders of the empire in Europe, the Middle East, and Africa had to be continually held against domestic insurrection and foreign invasion. Most of the legions were deployed at the outposts of the empire. More and more, the army's manpower was derived from conquered barbarians rather than Roman citizens.

In the 3rd and 4th centuries CE the army was again reorganized, first by the emperor Diocletian, and later by Constantine. The number of men in a legion was cut from 4,500 to 2,000 in order to gain mobility in fighting border wars. Total manpower was raised to 500,000, and discipline was strengthened. Constantine reorganized the legions into border guards and organized a mobile field army for a reserve force.

THE BYZANTINE EMPIRE

During the 5th and 6th centuries the western portion of the Roman Empire was overrun by invading barbarians. The center of power shifted to the Eastern, or Byzantine, Empire, with its capital at Constantinople. The Byzantine Empire was able to defend itself with a small, professional army consisting of barbarian mercenaries and landless peasants who volunteered as lifetime soldiers.

In the 7th century the Byzantine Empire reformed the army. It recruited citizens. These men were granted tracts of land to support their families. Over the years, the military families became powerful factions within the empire. The empire also brought the army under government control: the empire was divided into districts, and the viceroy of each district was made head of both the government and the army in his territory.

The emperor assumed the exclusive right to grant any military appointments. Prior to

The Barberini ivory, also called the Barberini diptych, depicts a Byzantine emperor emerging victorious after conquering adversaries. **DEA/G. Dagli Orti/De Agostini/Getty Images**

this time each general could reward his own men with promotions, money, and plunder.

The Byzantine army combined infantry and cavalry. Heavy cavalry, called cataphracts, wore iron helmets, shirts of metal scales called hauberks, and iron shoes. Their chief weapon was the bow and arrow, but they also fought with lance and broadsword. They carried no shields because both hands had to be free to shoot arrows. The Byzantine forces had the best medical service that was available in their time. Bearers carried the wounded out of battle to physicians behind the lines.

Little noticed at the time, but of great consequence for the makeup of armies, were some inventions that had originated in Persia and other eastern areas during the time of the Roman Republic. The stirrup, saddle, and horseshoe were devised. Also a new breed of large warhorse was developed. It became possible to mount a cavalryman wearing heavy armor and carrying heavier weapons. These innovations changed the nature of warfare in Europe until after the Middle Ages. Heavy cavalry came to dominate armies to such an extent that the use of foot soldiers became at times negligible.

CHAPTER 3

ARMIES IN THE MIDDLE AGES

The first fighters to make extensive use of the new horse power were the barbarians who invaded and eventually overran the Roman Empire in the West: the Goths, Huns, Vandals, and others. The end of this portion of the empire in the 4th and 5th centuries inaugurated the 1,000-year period called the Middle Ages. During this era, from approximately 476 to 1500, armies were almost continually on the march somewhere. Muslims, Mongols, and European states vied with each other for the control of territory, for trade routes, and for wealth and power. They also sought to spread their respective religions.

MUSLIM FORCES

The two most effective cavalry forces of the Middle Ages belonged to the Muslims and the Mongols. The Muslims, followers of the religion of Islam, expanded the influence of Islam during the Rashidun and Umayyad caliphates in the 7th and 8th centuries. Defensive and offensive battles were fought. All able-bodied men were obliged to serve in their armies.

The main Muslim force was the cavalry. The men wore helmets and mail and fought with swords, javelins, bows, daggers, and scimitars. The scimitar is a curved sword made of strong steel. Another vital weapon was the six-foot (1.8-m) pointed lance.

Only after encountering European armies did the Muslims realize that a strong infantry force such as the phalanx or legion was useful in war. For their foot soldiers they hired mercenaries, reserving the privilege of membership in the cavalry for Muslims.

Within 100 years after the death of Muhammad, their founder, in 632, Muslim armies had conquered the whole Middle East, all of North Africa, and Spain. The threat that they posed to Europe was finally turned back in 732 at the battle of Tours in France. They were defeated there by Charles Martel and his Frankish army.

THE MONGOLS

One of the best-trained and most disciplined armies the world has ever seen was that of the Mongols who swept across Asia and into Europe in the 13th century. Led by Genghis Khan, this army was virtually all cavalry, and the quality of their horsemanship was unmatched by any other army.

A Mongol force usually numbered 30,000 men in three *toumans*, or groups of 10,000. Each touman was divided into ten regiments of 1,000 men; each regiment into ten squadrons of 100; and each squadron into ten troops of ten men each. Under leaders like Genghis Khan and his general, Subotai, entire columns could travel great distances separately and reach the same battleground in time to fight.

Part of the Mongols' success can be attributed to the hardiness of the troops. They needed no supply train. The men could travel ten days while eating only a dried milk paste and drinking blood taken from each man's extra horse. The Mongols fought in a battle line five men deep. The first two lines, with helmets, leather breastplates, and small shields, attacked with lances and sabers. They used iron hooks to pull their opponents off their horses. The three back lines threw javelins and shot arrows; they wore no armor. Mongol commanders directed their men with black and white signal flags. Mongol

GENGHIS KHAN

From the high, windswept Gobi came one of history's most famous warriors. He was a Mongolian nomad known as Genghis Khan (1162?–1227). With his fierce, hard-riding nomad horde, he conquered a huge empire that stretched through Asia from the Yellow Sea to the Black Sea.

Genghis Khan was born on the Gobi, in a yurt, or felt tent, on a bank of the Onon River in northern Mongolia. His father, Yesügei, was the chief of several desert tribes and had just slain a foe named Temüjin. In triumph Yesügei named his newborn son Temüjin.

Yesügei died when Temüjin was nine years old. The boy succeeded him, but the fierce, restless nomads would not obey so young a chieftain. The chief of another tribe proclaimed himself leader of the Mongols and captured Temüjin. Guards forced Temüjin into a *kang*, a wooden yoke that shackled his shoulders and wrists. In the dark he slowly twisted himself to reach above a guard and smashed the kang down on his head. Then Temüjin raced to the river and escaped by hiding in water up to his chin.

Temüjin's bold courage and resourcefulness began to win followers. When he reached manhood, he conquered the Tatars and added them to his tribes. In 1203 he defeated the Keraits. Seizing their cities of mud and stone, he made Karakorum his capital.

In 1206 a council of his tribes named him Genghis Khan. It means "greatest of rulers, emperor of all men." Genghis Khan then put all his Mongolian realm under Yassa, a body of laws he assembled from

GENGHIS KHAN (CONTINUED)

various tribal codes. These laws demanded obedience to Genghis Khan, unity of the tribes, and pitiless punishment of wrongdoers. Through Yassa, Genghis Khan achieved the discipline that welded his wild tribesmen into merciless, successful armies.

On his march of conquest Genghis Khan over-ran north China from 1208 to 1215. Wheeling westward, his horde conquered Turkestan. Then his armies engulfed neighboring countries, even part of India. In 1222 the Mongols struck into Europe at the Don River. After defeating the Russians, they pushed to the Dnieper River. Victorious, Genghis Khan returned eastward. At his death his empire passed to his sons.

Mongol leader Genghis Khan. Popperfoto/Getty Images

armies conquered a vast empire stretching from China across Russia to the Middle East and Hungary.

FEUDAL ARMIES

During the same period in Western Europe, fighting was the business of mounted knights in armor. For most of the Middle Ages there were no standing armies in Europe. Military service was linked to owning land. Only big landowners could afford horses, armor, and weapons for themselves and their supporters, called men-at-arms. Small landowners became vassals (servants or tenants) of the more powerful. A vassal swore to fight and work for his lord in return for protection. The wealthiest men attracted many vassals and became more and more powerful. Even the wealthiest lords were vassals to a king, but it was difficult for a king to rule these powerful men.

A fully armed medieval knight wore a cylindrical helmet and a suit of mail. He carried a shield and fought with sword and lance. His horse had to be large enough to bear the weight of the armor and the shock of a lance thrust. Many young noblemen practiced horsemanship and the use of weapons from their youth.

Foot soldiers played no significant role during the Middle Ages. For one thing, they could not wear armor as heavy as that of mounted men, and so did not stand much chance against a charge by knights. Nor was much time spent drilling knights and foot soldiers in fighting together. In battle, foot soldiers were often trampled by the knights on their own side.

Vassals swore to fight for their lords 40 days every year. If a campaign lasted longer, many vassals simply went home. Medieval armies were cumbersome and poorly organized. Command was fragmented because vassals were loyal to their own lord first.

With the rise of strong kings and the development of new weapons such as the longbow (a wooden bow from five to six feet [1.5 to 1.8 m] long), the medieval army was gradually replaced by more disciplined forces. Kings allowed their vassals to contribute money instead of providing men. A king could then use the money to hire armies of mercenaries. In some states the native populations played no role in military campaigns.

CHANGING WEAPONRY AND FORMATIONS

As the Middle Ages were drawing to a close in the 14th and 15th centuries, the supremacy of the foot soldier began to reassert itself. This development was in part the result of improved weaponry that enabled infantry units to defeat cavalry.

In England infantrymen used the long-bow, which could shoot a yard-long arrow with great accuracy up to 200 yards (183 m). Trained English archers could fire six arrows a minute that could pierce a knight's armor. With the longbow an English army of 11,000 defeated a French army of 60,000 at Crécy, France, in 1346. The longbows drove back the slower-firing French crossbowmen, then shot down the knights' horses. Once the horses fell, it was a simple matter for the English to stab or club the clumsy armored knights. After the enemy line was broken, the English cavalry charged.

More important even than the longbow in the revival of infantry warfare was the renewed use of the Greek phalanx in modified forms. It was the Swiss who rediscovered the phalanx.

Comment le roy phelippe de
france fut desconfy en bataille

for sen vint logier a abewille
Ou ce soir il enhorta z reist

An illustration of the 1346 Battle of Crécy. The Bridgeman Art Library/
Getty Images

Unable, as a citizen army, to afford horses and armor, they contrived, through constant drill and good discipline, to learn how to maneuver and coordinate a mass of men in such a way as to defeat cavalry. The weapon that made this tactic feasible was the 19-foot (5.8-meter) pike carried by the first four ranks of the phalanx. While the pikemen speared charging horses, the troops behind them ran forward to attack the unhorsed knights.

The Swiss used three phalanxes, one behind the other. This prevented an enemy from outflanking the front lines. It also allowed the front phalanx to fall back into the one behind it for added strength. If surrounded, the Swiss formed a hedgehog, a hollow square with pikes pointing out on every side.

Innovations in weaponry during the late Middle Ages were to change the nature of warfare permanently. Firearms appeared in the late 14th century, and cannon were introduced in the 15th century. These weapons gradually made the pike, crossbow, longbow, and sword obsolete. They also promoted the infantry over the cavalry as a fighting force. Horses made better targets than men, and once the horseman was dismounted he had no advantage over the infantryman.

Between 1300 and 1648 the feudal system of Europe declined. The many social transformations that occurred significantly altered the makeup of armies. The breakdown of the vassal-master relationships forced kings, nobles, and city-state leaders to find other ways of raising armies. England turned to the citizen-soldier concept, while on the Continent the use of mercenaries became the standard method.

In England the practice of hiring foreign mercenaries was stopped by the Magna Carta of 1215. This document, limiting the powers of the monarchy, was imposed on King John by the nobles. The feudal system of calling up vassals proved unsatisfactory, for it often resulted in an untrained, undisciplined assemblage whose main thought was to get military service over with and go back to family and work. The outcome was that paid military service became the right and duty of all Englishmen. To fill out the army, specific numbers of men were drafted from each county for service in wartime.

THE RISE OF MERCENARY FORCES

On the Continent the decline of feudalism led to the hiring of mercenaries by kings and nobles alike. Even the city-states found it to their advantage to hire armies to fight their wars for them. The advantage of mercenaries over vassals was great: mercenaries were professional soldiers who devoted their whole lives to combat. This, in turn, led to war becoming a more professional and calculated affair on the part of kings and princes.

Groups of professional mercenaries banded together in what were called free companies to hire themselves out as units. The two most outstanding types of free companies were the *condottieri* (contractors) of Italy and the Swiss mercenaries. The condottieri were men who contracted for the services of units of mercenaries, then hired out units to princes for their wars. From the 13th through the 15th centuries, the condottieri and their troops monopolized warfare on the Italian peninsula. Their chief advantage was their professionalism; their main disadvantage was their lack of loyalty to a cause. Since they fought for money, they were frequently willing to change sides for higher pay.

The Swiss provided the best mercenary units in Europe. Their use of the phalanx and pikemen made them the champion fighters on the Continent. Every ruler in Europe wanted Swiss mercenaries in his army. These Swiss Guards, as they were also called, saw action in many wars from the 15th through the 19th centuries. In the 21st century the only remaining vestige of the Guards is the personal bodyguard of the pope in Vatican City. This Vatican Swiss Guard has been in existence since 1505.

In Germany, men called *landsknechts*, who were mercenaries, imitated the Swiss phalanx. After a time they became capable fighters.

Spain was the one state of Europe that did not use free-company fighters. The Spanish

The Swiss Guard standing in front of St. Peter's Basilica in Vatican City. Although only used now as the pope's bodyguard, between the 15th and 19th centuries, the Swiss Guards were among the best mercenaries in Europe. **Christopher Furlong/Getty Images**

armies, among the most powerful of the early modern period, consisted largely of mercenaries from Germany, The Netherlands, and Italy. These mercenaries were led by well-trained Spanish officers who infused them with a spirit of loyalty to Spain and its monarchs.

ARMIES FROM c. 1600 to 1945

The end of the Middle Ages is generally dated about 1500, but militarily it did not end until the time of the Thirty Years' War, fought from 1618 to 1648. By this time several strong nation-states had developed in Europe, among them France, Sweden, Spain, and the Holy Roman Empire consisting of the German states, Austria, and northern Italy. These monarchies had the manpower for large armies and the money to support them.

THE DEVELOPMENT OF STANDING ARMIES

The emergence of the national standing army comprised of citizen soldiers spelled the gradual decline in the wholesale use of mercenaries and free companies, although the tradition of the mercenary has persisted on a limited scale into the 21st century.

SWEDEN

Gustavus II Adolphus (1594–1632), king of Sweden, has been called the father of modern warfare. It was he who forged the first national standing army, one that was to be a model for other states for 150 years. All Swedish males over 15 years of age were drafted for military service. The forces he raised by conscription were augmented by mercenaries.

Gustavus organized the army into companies of 150 men. There were four companies in a battalion and three battalions in a brigade. To fight a battle, he arranged his infantry into regiments, each containing as many as ten companies, with the cavalry in front. The cavalry led the charge, while the infantry came forward behind them, stopping to fire and reload. The front row of the infantry fired from a kneeling position, while the next two fired standing. Prior to starting a battle, the artillery bombarded the enemy. This coordination of artillery, cavalry, and infantry was an innovation devised by Gustavus and soon adopted by other European armies.

To increase the mobility of his armies, Gustavus made improvements in weaponry. His soldiers used lighter muskets that could

Gustavus II Adolphus. Bob Thomas/Popperfoto/Getty Images

be loaded faster than previous models. Early muskets took two men to load and fire. The newer muskets were shorter and lighter. The powder charge was measured ahead of time and packed with the ball in a paper cartridge. The soldier had simply to bite off the end of the cartridge and ram the shot down the muzzle. Gustavus made similar improvements in his artillery. Heavy cannons were replaced with lighter ones that one horse could pull. Cannon shot was measured ahead of time. Supplies of powder, cannon balls, and musket shot were stored in depots all over the country so that the army did not have to carry excessive loads of ammunition.

During the Thirty Years' War, Gustavus taxed conquered districts to pay his soldiers. His armies were supplied with uniforms, weapons, food, and housing. His enemies, the armies of the Holy Roman Empire, had to find their own food and shelter in the lands they marched through; hence they lived by plunder and made enemies of local populations.

The first military leader to imitate the work of Gustavus Adolphus was Oliver Cromwell, during the English Civil War in the middle of the 17th century. His army was patterned after the Swedish army, and his only major innovation was the introduction of basic training for his troops.

PRUSSIA

After Gustavus Adolphus the next outstanding military genius of Europe was Frederick the Great, king of Prussia. He came to the throne in 1740 and ruled for 46 years. The first 23 years of his reign were spent in making Prussia a great military power and in fighting two major wars: the War of the Austrian Succession, from 1740 to 1745, and the Seven Years' War, from 1756 to 1763. Both of these wars were against Austria. Frederick's goal was the annexation of Silesia, a Polish province that had come under Austrian control in the 16th century. Frederick's greatest military strengths lay in enforcing strong discipline and in devising tactics. Frederick's father, Frederick William I, had raised the strength of the Prussian army to 80,000. Frederick increased this number to 140,000, then to 180,000. All young men of the lower classes could be drafted. Sons of the middle classes did not have to serve. Officers came from the class of nobles and wealthy landowners known as Junkers. The Prussian army consisted of infantry, cavalry, and artillery. The foot soldiers carried muskets with bayonets. By constant drilling they learned to load and fire their muskets five times a minute, while other armies could only do so twice a minute. This did not give the soldiers much time to aim, but careful aim did not matter, since the muskets were not accurate at more than 50 yards (45.7 m). Targets were not individual soldiers, but the mass of the enemy line.

Prussian soldiers assaulting an Austrian position in a churchyard in the Battle of Leuthen, Saxony, Dec. 5, 1757, during the Seven Years' War. Kean Collection/Archive Photos/Getty Images

The Prussian army formed a line three men deep. The line advanced until it was about 100 yards (91.4 m) from the enemy. The soldiers delivered a succession of volleys, then paced forward, reloading as they moved. When they came close to the enemy line, they charged with their bayonets.

On the flanks of the infantry rode the heavy cavalry in close formation. Its charges were carefully coordinated with the advance of the infantry to take advantage of any weakness in the enemy lines.

In his drill formations Frederick inaugurated the tactic of wheeling his line to change direction, thus enabling it to face an attack from a different direction. He also adopted the practice of arranging his line in echelon formation. This meant that a line would not be straight as it advanced, but each soldier, beginning with the second in line, would be at least one step behind the next. It would give the appearance of a diagonal line marching across a battlefield. The advantage of the echelon formation was that it exposed only one flank of his army.

The methods that Frederick the Great instituted in Prussia were adopted by the armies of Europe and the United States. His drill formations and tactics were used by most armies up through World War I. Modern mechanized warfare with airpower, tanks, and missiles has made them much less useful.

THE FRENCH REVOLUTION

What happened in France between the Revolution of 1789 and the defeat of Napoleon at Waterloo in 1815 was of far greater political than military significance. The Revolution began in 1789 as a class war. Within a few years the monarchy had been destroyed and class distinctions had been erased. Each person became a citizen of the reconstructed nation.

The import of what had happened in France was not lost upon the other monarchies of Europe. They saw this social upheaval as a threat to their very existence. The French were in part responsible because they wanted to spread their revolution to the rest of Europe. In response, Prussia and Austria formed a coalition to defeat the revolution and restore the monarchy.

With the monarchy gone, the immediate reaction of the French was to identify defense of the revolution with defense of the nation.

For the first time in history, all the loyalties and aspirations of a people were bound up with the fate of their country. Modern patriotism was born: a nation would go to arms to defend itself. A new relationship had been forged between a state and its army, a relationship that has played a vital role in most nations since the 19th century.

France's call to arms in 1793 brought forth more than one million men, the first army of such size in modern times. The revolutionary government decreed that every citizen—young or old, man or woman—was to work for victory against the Austrian-Prussian coalition by making ammunition, providing and moving supplies, and nursing the wounded. War was no longer left to the professionals; the day of the citizen soldier had arrived. To raise its armies, the French used conscription, a practice that soon was to spread to the rest of Europe.

NAPOLEON

Napoleon was the general who welded the French armies into a combat force that defeated the other armies of Europe for 20 years, from 1795 to 1815. His division contained infantry, artillery, and cavalry. He assembled two or three divisions into a corps to make larger units for battle.

Napoleon had two main strategies: he sought out terrain most favorable to his armies to fight on, and he used artillery and masses of men to breach the enemy's weakest point and disrupt its battle plans. His methods were normally direct and simple: use a fast-moving army to breach the

Three plans for the Battle of Waterloo, where Napoleon was defeated and 23 years of warfare between France and other European powers came to an end. **Hulton Archive/Getty Images**

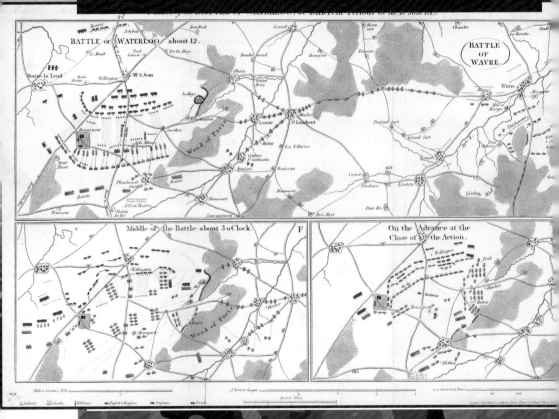

enemy lines, then outmaneuver and out-flank them. Napoleon was finally defeated at Waterloo, Belgium, because the armies of the Prussians and the English had learned to use some of his own tactics and employed them against him.

THE 19TH CENTURY

In the history of armies, the 19th century covers the period from Napoleon's defeat at Waterloo in June 1815 to the start of World War I in August 1914. The two features that stand out in this period are the great strides in technology and invention and the major organizational changes made in armies.

The Industrial Revolution of the 18th and 19th centuries brought with it improvements in manufacturing such as the assembly line and interchangeable parts. This meant that weapons would be made more rapidly and they could be standardized. The use of steel instead of cast iron or bronze meant that rifles, revolvers, and cannon were of better quality and more durable.

In addition to weaponry, there were a number of other inventions and new processes that had an impact on the way armies fought. The canning and refrigerating of food made feeding armies easier. The invention of the steamship, railroad, telegraph, telephone, lightbulb, automobile, airplane, and tank changed warfare markedly between 1815 and the end of World War I by improving transportation, communication, and combat effectiveness.

In terms of organization, few changes were made in European armies and none in the United States Army in the first half of the 19th century. The unification of Germany under Otto von Bismarck in the 1860s caused a complete change in the military situation, however. In the next few decades Europe became an armed camp. Every nation of any size instituted conscription and greatly increased the size of its army. Large reserve forces were also built up. Germany, for instance, increased the size of its army from 400,000 to 850,000 and kept a reserve of more than 4 million in the period immediately before World War I. France, Austria, and Russia followed a similar course. The exception was Britain, essentially a naval power until the World War made conscription necessary.

THE AMERICAN CIVIL WAR

While the nations of Europe were arming themselves and reorganizing their land forces, the greatest conflict of the century was fought across the Atlantic. The American Civil War (also called the War Between the States in the South), fought from 1861 to 1865, has been called the first modern war. It was a gigantic struggle in which more than 617,000 died and at least 375,000 were wounded. The theater of war was 1,500 miles (2,414 km) wide from east to west, and 800 miles (1,287 km) from north to south. It was the first war in which railroads, telegraph, ironclad ships, torpedoes, and modern breech-loading rifles were used. It was a war in which the industrial might of one side, the North, was able to wear down and defeat a largely agricultural economy, the South.

The number of soldiers who fought in the war was huge. There were about 2,375,000 in the Union armies of the North and 900,000 in the Southern Confederacy over the course of the war. Most of these men were volunteers, along with a few thousand professional soldiers from the regular army. The commanders on both sides were officers trained at

Union soldiers in an artillery battery during the Civil War. Archive Photos/Getty Images

the military academy of West Point. Infantry regiments numbered 1,000 men, and cavalry units were about the same size. Artillery batteries were small in size at the start of the war—usually about six guns—but by the end of the war they had been organized into brigades of five batteries to increase concentration of fire power at key points on the large fronts in most battles.

Two aspects of Civil War battles are notable because they were to become standard procedures in World War I: entrenchment and advance. For the first time in warfare the construction of hasty field fortifications and trenches before battle became customary. When a battle began, the cavalry and infantry of both sides charged forward.

The infantry, as the war dragged on, adopted the tactic of advance by rush: half the men would fire at the enemy while standing still, and the other half ran ahead. Then that half would stop and fire while the others in turn rushed the enemy. Cavalry soldiers of the North usually dismounted to fight, while those of the South remained on horseback.

The size and complexity of the Civil War made it necessary for both the Union and the Confederacy to increase the size of their staff systems. Neither side had a staff like the general staffs of the nations of Europe. In the course of the war there were advances in military engineering because of the need to build bridges, fortifications, and entrenchments.

Other wars were fought between 1815 and 1914: the Crimean War (1854–56), the Franco-Prussian War (1870), the Boer War (1899–1902), the Russo-Japanese War (1904–5), and the Balkan Wars (1912–13). None was of the magnitude of the American Civil War.

Yet the military establishments of Europe and Japan were not disposed to learn much from the Americans. The Europeans and the Japanese considered the American Civil War to be a conflict between amateur armies and therefore tended to ignore its tactics.

WORLD WARS

The failure of the Europeans to learn from the American Civil War led them to fight the same kind of war in World War I as they always had fought. The armies of Europe, and finally, of the United States, fought for four years, only to end in a stalemate. Nothing was settled despite massive loss of life.

WORLD WAR I

Some of the tactics used in the First World War were much the same as those used in the American Civil War: principally, the building of fortifications and digging of trenches before charging the enemy with rifle fire and the falling back to the trenches if no gain was made.

The armies of World War I were the largest put into the field up to that time. The Germans were able to mobilize 2 million men in two days, and within five days about 1 million soldiers were on the march toward France. Austria mobilized 500,000 men, while France started out with 1,600,000; Russia called up an army of 1,400,000; Great Britain, with the only all-volunteer army in Europe, had only 120,000 at the start of the war.

By 1917 the British Army had increased tenfold; the French land forces had been enlarged to 2,600,000; and in 1918 the American Army in France numbered 1,200,000. It was the addition of troops from the United States that made it possible to defeat German forces numbering about 2.5 million.

Army organization for all the belligerents remained the same as it had been throughout the 19th century. They all had similar infantry and cavalry divisions, artillery brigades, engineering companies, supply units, and medical units.

The advances in technology that had been made since the American Civil War were not sufficient to tip the balance either way. Both sides made use of airplanes, tanks, radio, machine guns, and other inventions. The newness of these technologies meant that they had to be adapted to wartime use on a trial-and-error basis. Many inventions were developed for commercial use, such as the

TRENCH WARFARE

Trench warfare is warfare in which opposing armed forces attack, counterattack, and defend from relatively permanent systems of trenches dug into the ground. The opposing systems of trenches are usually close to one another. Trench warfare is resorted to when the superior firepower of the defense compels the opposing forces to "dig in" so extensively as to sacrifice their mobility in order to gain protection.

Soldiers of the British Army in a trench in Givenchy, France, during World War I. Hulton Archive/Getty Images

Trench warfare reached its highest development on the Western Front during World War I (1914–18), when armies of millions of men faced each other in a line of trenches extending from the Belgian coast through northeastern France to Switzerland. These trenches arose within the first few months of the war's outbreak, after the great offensives launched by Germany and France had shattered against the deadly, withering fire of the machine gun and the rapid-firing artillery piece. The sheer quantity of bullets and shells flying through the air in the battle conditions of that war compelled soldiers to burrow into the soil to obtain shelter and survive.

The typical trench system in World War I consisted of a series of two, three, four, or more trench lines running parallel to each other and being at least 1 mile (1.6 km) in depth. Each trench was dug in a type of zigzag so that no enemy, standing at one end, could fire for more than a few yards down its length. Each of the main lines of trenches was connected to each other and to the rear by a series of communications trenches that were dug roughly perpendicular to them. Food, ammunition, fresh troops, mail, and orders were delivered through these trenches. The intricate network of trenches contained command posts, forward supply dumps, first-aid stations, kitchens, and latrines. Most importantly, it had machine-gun emplacements to defend against an assault, and it had dugouts deep enough to shelter large numbers of defending troops during an enemy bombardment.

telephone, radio, and internal-combustion engine, and were only gradually adapted for use in warfare. It was not until World War II that full advantage was taken of the technologies of mechanized warfare.

INTERWAR PERIOD

The interwar period, from 1918 to 1939, was marked by a feeling of revulsion to all war on the part of most of the belligerents. The armies of the Allies—France, Britain, and the United States—were all drastically reduced in size. Only Germany differed in these matters. Convinced that their country had been betrayed by its politicians in World War I, the Germans continued to prepare secretly for another conflict. Russia, allied with France against Germany, had been knocked out of the conflict by the Revolution of 1917 and a hastily arranged treaty with the new Communist government.

The gravest mistake made by the former Allies between 1919 and 1939 was the failure of the military to keep up with industrial development and new technologies. The one change that was made was the addition of air force auxiliaries to the several armies.

While Germany was secretly modifying its industries for rapid changeover to wartime production, the other nations were convinced a war could not occur again. When war did come in 1939, the Allies had to make very rapid changes in their industrial capacity to meet the German challenge. They also were forced to use conscription.

WORLD WAR II

Civil war in Spain from 1936 to 1939 provided a small-scale dress rehearsal for World War II. Volunteers from other countries went to Spain to fight. Soldiers on leave from Germany and Italy went to fight on the side of Francisco Franco. Americans, Canadians, Englishmen, and others went to fight for the Spanish republic. Italy and Germany, both dictatorships and both preparing for war, had a chance to try out their new airplanes and tanks as well as other weapons. Tanks were used for frontal attack and airplanes for the strafing of infantry and for bombing missions.

During the early decades of the 20th century a great military power emerged in the Far East. Japan had for some decades been mobilizing all of its industrial and human resources to increase the strength of its armed forces. By 1941, when Japan entered World War II, it had built up an army of about 55 infantry divisions and 35 tank regiments. Its army air force had about 1,600 combat planes.

World War II, fought from 1939 to 1945, had several characteristics that distinguished it from World War I: the coordination of all services—armies, air forces, and navies—in one common effort; the use of amphibious (combined land–sea operations) warfare; the coordination of tanks and airplanes in initial attacks (a tactic the Germans called blitzkrieg, meaning "lightning warfare"); and the use of radio communications among areas, both in the air and on the ground. It was the first fully mechanized war. The cavalry, which had been part of armies for hundreds of years, was finally obsolete. The term "cavalry," however, continued to be used to describe mechanized units.

More combatants were mobilized for World War II than at any previous time. For the major belligerents the total number of fighting men in all services was: Australia, 1,000,000; Canada, 1,041,080; China, 17,250,521; Germany, 20,000,000; Great Britain, 5,896,000; Italy, 3,100,000; Japan, 9,700,000; the Soviet Union (army only), 12,000,000; the United States, 11,000,000; and Yugoslavia, 3,741,000.

The organization of armies changed very little from the prewar period. Divisions numbered from 11,000 to 15,000 men, depending on national policy. Airborne divisions numbered from 6,000 to 10,000. The major change was in the number of backup and support troops such as engineers, signal troops, supply troops, mechanics, communications experts, and medical personnel. For the first time, women served in uniform in fairly large numbers. They did administrative and communications work and performed many other support functions.

The command structures of the armies remained as they had been before the war, but there were two innovations in the scope

Members of the Auxiliary Territorial Service, the women's branch of the British Army during World War II, line up for inspection by Queen Mary. Hulton Archive/Getty Images

of command. For the first time, joint and combined commands were used. Joint commands meant placing all of the armed services of a nation—army, navy, and air force—under a single command in a theater of operations. Combined command involved two or more nations. For example, Gen. Dwight D. Eisenhower of the United States was supreme commander of all Allied forces operating in Europe. World War II was brought to an end by the dropping of atom bombs on two Japanese cities, Hiroshima and Nagasaki, in the summer of 1945. With the dawn of the atomic, or nuclear, age, military personnel and civilians alike at first believed that the nature of warfare had been changed forever. This did not prove to be the case. All the major nations of the world maintain standing armies, and conventional weapons—albeit highly sophisticated—are still used. Many more or less conventional wars have been fought since 1945, including conflicts in Vietnam, Korea, and the Middle East.

ARMED CONFLICT SINCE 1945

In the wake of the most devastating conflict in human history, the world's two superpowers—the United States and the Soviet Union—settled into an uneasy peace. The second half of the 20th century would see these two nations engage in a series of proxy wars, as the Soviets sought to expand their sphere of influence, while the United States pursued a policy known as containment. Containment, a strategy proposed by U.S. diplomat George Kennan in 1947, involved the economic and military support of anticommunist regimes. The two most conspicuous examples of this policy were the wars in Korea and Vietnam. Major armed conflicts of the late 20th and early 21st centuries include the wars in Iraq and Afghanistan.

KOREAN WAR

In June 1950 North Korea invaded South Korea with a force of more than 100,000 men armed with Soviet equipment. U.S.

Pres. Harry Truman ordered troops to assist South Korea. The United Nations Security Council, minus the absent Soviet delegate, passed a resolution calling for the assistance of all United Nations (UN) members in halting the North Koreans. At first North Korean troops drove the South Korean and U.S. forces down to the southern tip of the Korean peninsula, but a brilliant amphibious landing at Inch'ŏn, conceived by Gen. Douglas MacArthur, turned the tide in favor of the UN troops, who advanced near the border of North Korea and China. By this time, combat troops under UN command numbered in excess of 400,000.

China then entered the war with a force of some 300,000 and drove the UN forces back south. Throughout the war, the Chinese adhered to a formula for fighting UN forces: attack at night, cut off routes of supply and withdrawal, ambush counterattacking forces, and exploit all forms of concealment and cover. The front line stabilized at the 38th parallel. MacArthur insisted on voicing his objections to U.S. war aims in a public manner and was relieved of his command by Truman. U.S. Pres. Dwight D. Eisenhower participated in the conclusion of an armistice in July 1953 that accepted the front line as the de facto boundary between the two Koreas. The war resulted in the deaths of approximately 2,000,000 Koreans, 600,000 Chinese, 37,000 Americans, and 3,000 Turks, Britons, and other nationals in the UN forces. Although the armistice brought a close to open hostilities, the two Koreas remained technically at war, and the demilitarized zone (DMZ) that separated the two countries was one of the world's most heavily fortified borders.

VIETNAM WAR

After the First Indochina War (1946-54), Vietnam was partitioned into North Vietnam and South Vietnam to separate the warring parties until free elections could be held in 1956. In the North leader Ho Chi Minh's popular—and communist-sympathizing— Viet Minh party was expected to win the elections, which the leader in the South, Ngo Dinh Diem, refused to hold. In the war that ensued, fighters trained by North Vietnam (the Viet Cong) fought a guerrilla war against U.S.-supported South Vietnamese forces; North Vietnamese forces later joined the fighting. Most "battles" of the war were sharp, very brief engagements between units

GUERRILLA WARFARE

One major factor armies have had to deal with since World War II is guerrilla warfare. The term "guerrilla" means "little war"; it is a type of warfare characterized by fighting limited actions, often on terrain difficult for a regular army to dominate. Guerrillas use hit-and-run tactics, sabotage, terrorism, and propaganda. They are highly mobile, use unorthodox methods, obtain weapons from any available source, and normally live off the country without regular supply lines. Many of the wars and revolutions since 1945 have involved guerrilla warfare: particularly notable were the Cuban Revolution of 1959, the Vietnam War (1954–75), and the wars in Afghanistan (1978–92; 2001–).

Members of the Viet Cong advance as others fire machine guns. Viet Cong soldiers employed a variety of guerrilla tactics during the Vietnam War. Three Lions/Hulton Archive/Getty Images

of fewer than 200 men, and the massive U.S. advantage in firepower was largely countered by the ability of the North Vietnamese to disappear into the jungle or the civilian population.

At the height of U.S. involvement, there were more than half a million U.S. military personnel in Vietnam. The Tet Offensive of 1968, in which the Viet Cong and North Vietnamese attacked 36 of 44 South Vietnamese provincial capitals and 64 district capitals, marked a turning point in the war. Many in the U.S. had come to oppose the war on moral and practical grounds, and Pres. Lyndon B. Johnson decided to shift to a policy of de-escalation. Beginning in 1969 U.S. troops were withdrawn from Vietnam, but the war was expanded to Cambodia and Laos in 1970. Peace talks, which had reached a stalemate in 1971, started again in 1973, producing a cease-fire agreement; the last U.S. military unit left Vietnam later that year.

Fighting continued, and there were numerous truce violations. In 1975 the North Vietnamese launched a full-scale invasion of the South. The South surrendered later that year, and in 1976 the country was reunited as the Socialist Republic of Vietnam. More than 3,000,000 people (including 58,000

Americans, more than 4,000 South Koreans, more than 500 Australians, and about 350 Thai) died over the course of the war, more than half of them civilians.

PERSIAN GULF WAR

On Aug. 2, 1990, Iraq invaded the small oil-rich country of Kuwait. Though justified by Iraqi leader Ṣaddām Ḥussein on grounds that Kuwait was historically part of Iraq, the invasion was presumed to be motivated by Iraq's desire to acquire Kuwait's oil fields and to expand its power in the region. The United States, fearing Iraq's broader strategic intentions and acting under UN auspices, formed a broad coalition, which included a number of Arab countries, and began massing troops in northern Saudi Arabia.

When Iraq ignored a UN Security Council deadline for it to withdraw from Kuwait, the coalition began a large-scale air offensive code-named Operation Desert Storm (Jan. 16–17, 1991). Ṣaddām responded by launching ballistic missiles against neighboring coalition states as well as Israel. The F-117 stealth fighter and the Patriot missile defense system were conspicuous additions to the U.S. arsenal during this period of the war. A ground offensive by the coalition (Feb. 24–28) achieved victory with such speed that one U.S. general observed that Iraq had gone from the fourth largest army in the world to the second largest army in Iraq in 100 hours. Estimates of Iraqi military deaths range up to 100,000; coalition forces lost about 300 troops. As the Iraqi military made use of Soviet weapons and doctrine, its rapid defeat led to a dramatic reexamination of the effectiveness of such systems and tactics.

AFGHANISTAN WAR

Within weeks of the hijacking of four jetliners by operatives of the militant Islamist organization al-Qaeda on Sept. 11, 2001, the U.S. began military operations in Afghanistan, where al-Qaeda had been hosted by the Taliban regime. Teams of commandos infiltrated the country to coordinate with Afghan anti-Taliban groups while a U.S. bombing campaign weakened the Taliban, allowing anti-Taliban forces to take control of the country by December.

As Taliban leaders retreated into rural areas and into Pakistan, an interim Afghan government was formed, and more U.S. troops, along with forces representing

A Taliban fighter in Afghanistan. Over 40 Taliban fighters surrendered their weapons following a government operation in Herat Province in 2009. Majid Saeedi/Getty Images

the North Atlantic Treaty Organization (NATO), arrived to stabilize the country. In spite of promises for a large-scale rebuilding effort, American attention and resources were quickly diverted to the Iraq War, leaving reconstruction in Afghanistan underfunded and plagued by waste and corruption.

By 2005 a Pashtun insurgency had emerged, led by a reconstituted Taliban. Attacks were concentrated in eastern Afghanistan, where fighters were able to use the tribal areas of western Pakistan as a rear base. Faced with increasing violence, the U.S. began secretly targeting militants in Pakistan with missiles fired from remotely piloted drones in 2007.

The U.S. sent an additional 30,000 troops to Afghanistan in late 2009 and increased the pace of drone strikes in an effort to slow the insurgency. In May 2011 al-Qaeda leader Osama bin Laden was killed by U.S. special forces operatives in Abbottabad, Pak., and the following month, the U.S. announced a plan calling for the withdrawal of combat troops from Afghanistan by 2014.

Iraq War

U.S. Pres. George W. Bush argued that the September 11, 2001, attacks on the U.S. highlighted the threat to U.S. security posed by hostile countries such as Iraq. Bush and British Prime Minister Tony Blair declared in early 2003 that Iraq was hindering UN inspections and that it still retained proscribed weapons of mass destruction (WMD). On March 20, 2003, a U.S.-led coalition launched a series of air attacks on Iraq, and a ground invasion followed. Iraqi forces were rapidly defeated, and on April 9 U.S. forces took control of the capital, Baghdad. British forces completed their occupation of the southern city of Basra the same day. On May 1 major combat operations were completed, and that December, U.S. forces captured Iraqi Pres. Ṣaddām Ḥussein, who had been in hiding since the fall of Baghdad.

The U.S. and other occupying forces were soon embroiled in escalating guerrilla warfare that hindered Iraq's recovery and killed thousands of soldiers and tens of thousands of civilians. The war, long opposed by many throughout the world, also became increasingly unpopular in the U.S., as it became clear that Iraq did not, in fact, possess weapons of mass destruction. Sectarian fighting and insurgent attacks on U.S. and Iraqi forces peaked in 2006 and 2007. Improvised explosive devices (IEDs) such as roadside bombs were used to brutal effect by insurgents, ultimately accounting for some two-thirds of coalition casualties in Iraq.

In early 2007 the U.S. implemented a strategy that came to be known as the "surge," which consisted of temporarily increasing the number of troops in Iraq by more than 20,000 in a bid to stabilize the country. By the end of the year, violence had decreased substantially, although the role of the surge in improving security remained a source of debate. In 2008 the U.S. began to gradually reduce the number of its troops in Iraq, completing its withdrawal in December 2011.

CHAPTER 6

NOTABLE ARMIES OF THE MODERN AGE

Advances in technology have made modern armies faster, smarter, and, potentially, far more destructive than their forbears. A modern mechanized infantry soldier can travel hundreds of miles in a single day, utilizing imagery from satellites or unmanned aerial vehicles to command a bird's eye view of the battlefield. Additionally, modern small arms confer upon a single individual a rate of fire that rivals that of an entire early 20th-century rifle platoon. A survey of armies from some of the more historically volatile regions of the world illustrates the impact of changing technologies and reveals varying security priorities across countries from the second half of the 20th century through the modern age.

CHINA

The People's Liberation Army (PLA) is the unified organization of all Chinese land, sea, and air forces. The history of the PLA is officially traced to the Nanchang Uprising of Aug. 1, 1927, which is celebrated annually as PLA Day. The PLA is one of the world's largest military forces, with more than 2 million members. Military service is compulsory for all men who attain the age of 18; women may register for duty in the medical, veterinary, and other technical services.

Demobilized servicemen are carried in a ready reserve, which is reinforced by a standby reserve of veterans and by the militia. The PLA is formally under the command of the Central Military Commission

Members of the PLA reserve force at a ceremony in Nanjing, China.
China Photos/Getty Images

CYBERWAR

Cyberwar is war conducted in and from computers and the networks connecting them, waged by states or their proxies against other states. Cyberwar is usually waged against government and military networks in order to disrupt, destroy, or deny their use. Cyberwar should not be confused with the terrorist use of cyberspace or with cyberespionage or cybercrime. Even though similar tactics are used in all four types of activities, it is a misinterpretation to define them all as cyberwar. Some states that have engaged in cyberwar may also have engaged in disruptive activities such as cyberespionage, but such activities in themselves do not constitute cyberwar.

Computers and the networks that connect them are collectively known as the domain of cyberspace. Western states depend on cyberspace for the everyday functioning of nearly all aspects of modern society, and developing states are becoming more reliant upon cyberspace every year. Everything modern society needs to function—from critical infrastructures and financial institutions to modes of commerce and tools for national security—depends to some extent upon cyberspace. Therefore, the threat of cyberwar and its purported effects are a source of great concern for governments and militaries around the world, and several serious cyberattacks have taken place that, while not necessarily meeting a strict definition of cyberwar, can serve as an illustration of what might be expected in a real cyberwar of the future.

The term "cyberwar" is increasingly controversial. A number of experts in the fields of computer security and international politics question whether the term accurately characterizes the hostile activity occurring in cyberspace. Many suggest that the activities in question can be more accurately described as crime, espionage, or even terrorism but not necessarily as war, since the latter term has important political, legal, and military implications. For example, it is far from apparent that an act of espionage by one state against another via cyberspace equals an act of war—just as traditional methods of espionage have rarely, if ever, led to war. Allegations of Chinese cyberespionage bear this out. A number of countries, including India, Germany, and the United States, believe that they have been victims of Chinese cyberespionage efforts. Nevertheless, while these incidents have been a cause of tension between China and the other countries, they have not damaged overall diplomatic relations.

Such qualifications aside, it is widely believed that cyberwar not only will feature prominently in all future conflicts but will probably even constitute the opening phases of them. The role and prominence of cyberwar in conventional conflicts continues to escalate.

of the Chinese Communist Party. Troops around the country are stationed in seven military regions and more than 20 military districts. Despite the drive to modernize the PLA, limited military budgets and other constraints have caused the sophistication of conventional military armaments and of logistics and command-and-control systems to lag behind that of other major military powers. Intelligence officials and computer security analysts have agreed, however, that the PLA has maintained a robust and active cyberwar and industrial espionage program that has targeted foreign corporations and governments.

EGYPT

Egypt maintains one of the largest and strongest military forces in the Middle East, with over 450,000 troops under its command. Roughly three-fourths of its overall military strength is in the army. As part of the peace process with Israel, the United States has provided the country with large amounts of military aid, and the army is equipped with large numbers of state-of-the-art main battle tanks along with field artillery and other armored equipment.

Most importantly, Egypt is one of the few in the region with its own military industrial complex. Egyptian firms connected with the government manufacture light armored vehicles and missiles (short and medium range) and assemble some of their heavy armored vehicles under contracts with foreign firms.

The officer corps has traditionally played a prominent role in politics. There are a number of paramilitary units, which are mostly responsible for internal security. The largest of these, the Central Security Forces (CSF), reports to the Ministry of the Interior and maintains troop strength nearly as high as the army. As is the case with many countries of the region, the intelligence services are ubiquitous and play an important role in internal security. Both the military and paramilitary services rely on conscription to fill their ranks, with the service obligation for males beginning at age 18. An additional period of service in the military reserve is generally required after discharge.

IRAN

Under the monarchy, Iran had one of the largest armed forces in the world, but it quickly dissolved with the overthrow of the shah in 1979. Reconstituted following the revolution, the Iranian military engaged in a protracted war with Iraq (1980–88) and has since maintained a formidable active and reserve component.

Since the mid-1980s Iran has sought to establish programs to develop weapons of mass destruction, including nuclear, biological, and chemical weapons (Iran used the latter in its war with Iraq), and by the late 1990s it had achieved some success in the domestic production of medium- and intermediate-range missiles—effective from 300 to 600 miles (480 to 965 km) and from 600 to 3,300 miles (965 to 5,310 km) away, respectively.

Iran's military obtains much of its manpower from conscription, and males are required to serve 21 months of military service. The army is the largest branch of Iran's military, numbering some 350,000 men, followed by the Revolutionary Guards, which accounts for an additional 125,000 men. This body, organized in the republic's early days, is the country's most effective military force and consists of the most politically dependable and religiously devout personnel. Any security forces that are involved in external war or in armed internal conflict are either accompanied or led by elements of the Revolutionary Guards. A Revolutionary Guards unit known as the al-Quds Force specializes in unconventional warfare and special operations outside of Iran.

ISRAEL

The Israel Defense Forces (IDF) doctrine has been shaped since Israel's founding by the country's need to stave off attack from the numerically superior and geographically advantaged forces of its hostile Arab neighbors. This doctrine encompasses the IDF's belief that Israel cannot afford to lose a single war, a goal that it feels can be attained only through a defensive strategy that includes a peerless intelligence community and early warning systems. Additionally Israel maintains a well-trained, rapidly mobilized reserve component combined with a strategic capability that consists of a small, highly trained, active-duty force that can take the war to the enemy, quickly attain military objectives, and rapidly reduce hostile forces.

An integrated organization encompassing sea, air, and land forces, the IDF consists of a small corps of career officers, active-duty conscripts, and reservists. Military service is compulsory for Jews and Druze, both men and women, and for Circassian men. The period of active-duty conscription is three

Armored personnel carriers and tanks of the Israeli Army leave the northern Gaza Strip after an operation in 2007. David Furst/AFP/Getty Images

years for men and two for women; this is followed by a decades-long period of compulsory reserve duty (to age 50 for women and age 55 for men). Since the IDF depends on the reserve service of the population to meet manpower requirements, it continues to be mainly a popular militia rather than a professional army. In addition, a special force, the

Nahal, combines military and agricultural training and is also responsible for establishing new defense settlements along Israel's borders.

NORTH KOREA

North Korea strongly emphasizes military preparedness, and economic plans have been tailored to support high military expenditures. With the start of the Kim Jong Il regime in 1998 a policy of "military first politics" was put in place; it enshrined a strong military as the guardian of North Korea's accomplishments and the key component of its economic and political power, thus prioritizing it above other concerns of state. Although the bulk of its battlefield weaponry is several generations out of date and chronic fuel shortages limit the country's mechanized capabilities, North Korea claims to have more than 10,000 artillery pieces trained on the Southern capital of Seoul, and it regards chemical agents as a standard battlefield weapon.

North Korea maintains one of the world's largest military organizations, with more than 1 million men and women in uniform. The country's reserve and paramilitary forces bolster this number by more than 6 million.

All men and a limited number of women are subject to conscription. The duration of service officially is three to four years but typically lasts longer depending on the branch of service.

THE SOVIET UNION AND RUSSIA

With 5,081,000 members in the late 1980s, the Soviet Union's Army was second only to China's in size. This huge force was deployed within all the major regions of the Soviet Union itself, as well as in the satellite nations of Eastern Europe.

The Red Army was founded in January 1918, shortly after the Russian Revolution. Conscription was introduced, and by 1936 the Army numbered more than 1.5 million. Between 1936 and 1939 tens of thousands of Army officers were executed in Joseph Stalin's political purges. Following this disaster the Army was reorganized by Marshal K.E. Voroshilov and proved itself a worthy instrument in the defeat of Germany in World War II.

Following the war more reorganization was undertaken, and the name Red Army was replaced by Soviet Army. Command was placed under the Ministry of Defense headed by a civilian official. The Ministry was responsible to the Presidium of the Supreme Soviet, which was the governing body of the Soviet Union. Each branch of the armed services had its own military commander in chief. With the fall of Communism and the collapse of the Soviet Union in 1991, the newly formed Commonwealth of Independent States and the individual republics began negotiations to determine who would gain control of the armed forces.

More than two decades after the collapse of the Soviet Union, the Russian army remained a body in transition. About half its troops are conscripts: military service, lasting 18 months for the army or 24 months for the navy, is compulsory for men over age 18, although draft evasion is widespread. In a typical year, more than 1 million men are in active service, with many million more available as reserves.

In the 1990s controversy arose over attempts to reduce the size of the armed forces and create a professional military by abolishing conscription. This topic was revived in the early 21st century, as reformers sought to modernize outdated doctrines and command structures. Russia maintains defense facilities in several former Soviet republics and contributes a small proportion of its troops to the joint forces of the Commonwealth of Independent States. Russia's military capacity has declined since the breakup of the Soviet Union, a fact that Pres. Vladimir Putin sought to address by dramatically increasing defense spending from 2010–13. Nonetheless, it still has one of the world's largest armed forces establishments, which includes a vast nuclear arsenal.

THE UNITED STATES ARMY

As the commander in chief of the armed forces, the president of the United States maintains civilian control over the Army. The Department of the Army is a branch of the cabinet-level Department of Defense, which is headed by a civilian secretary who is appointed by the president. The secretary of the Army, also a civilian appointed by the president, is under the authority of the secretary of defense and of the president.

Civilian control of the Army is also maintained by the United States Congress through its reviews of Army programs and its appropriations. Each house of Congress has an Armed Services Committee.

The top military officer of the Army is the Army chief of staff, a four- or five-star general appointed by the president. Along with the heads of the Air Force, and Navy, the Army chief of staff is a member of the Joint Chiefs of Staff, who serve as the principal military advisers to the secretary of defense and to the president. The Army chief of staff is assisted by an inspector general and an auditor general and by a policy committee on the Army Reserve forces.

The Army General Staff consists of a comptroller and of offices of operations and plans; personnel; logistics; research, development, and acquisition; intelligence; and automation and communications. Special Staff agencies include the offices of the adjutant general, chief of engineers, surgeon general, chief of chaplains, and judge advocate general. The chiefs of the Army Reserve forces and of the National Guard Bureau are also members of the Special Staff.

ORGANIZATION

The active United States Army, which is made up of the officers and the enlisted men and women who are on active duty, is one of the three parts of the total Army. The other two are the Army Reserve and the Army National Guard.

The Army Reserve is made up of civilians, many of whom also hold full-time jobs. The Army Reserve is divided into three categories: the Ready Reserve, forces available for immediate mobilization; the Standby

Reserve, forces available in times of national emergency; and the Retired Reserve, which is comprised of retired troops who, in general, can be recalled prior to their 60th birthdays.

Although the Army Reserve has several designated combat units, most of its units provide the Active Army with combat support during national emergencies. The Army Reserve also assumes important training responsibilities in times of crisis.

The Army National Guard is the oldest military force in the United States. It traces its origins to the trained bands in the

Soldiers of the United States Army Reserve stand at attention on the west front of the Capitol in Washington, D.C., during a ceremony honoring the 100th anniversary of the branch. **Tom Williams/CQ-Roll Call Group/ Getty Images**

Massachusetts Bay Colony that date from 1636. There are Army National Guard units in all 50 states, the District of Columbia, Puerto Rico, and the United States Virgin Islands. Most Army National Guard members are assigned to combat units.

The Army National Guard is both a federal and a state military force. The governors of the states command the Army National Guard during peacetime. Units of the Army National Guard often assist state or local officials in dealing with natural disasters and civil disorders. On the order of the president, the Army National Guard can be called to federal duty and its units made part of the Active Army.

The Army's responsibilities are divided among 3 Army Commands (ACOM), 9 Army Service Component Commands (ASCC), and 11 Directly Reporting Units (DRU), all organized under the headquarters of the Department of the Army.

The United States Army Forces Command (FORSCOM) is an ACOM that supervises Active Army and Army Reserve troops in the continental United States. Headquartered at Fort Bragg, N.C., the command oversees the bulk of the Army's operational force. The Army Forces Command is also in charge of the training of units of the Army National Guard. Other responsibilities include the development of plans for mobilization.

The United States Army Training and Doctrine Command (TRADOC) is an ACOM that directs combat training programs for forces of both the Active Army and the Army Reserve. It is headquartered at Fort Eustis, Va.

The United States Army Materiel Command (AMC) is an ACOM in charge of the equipment used by the Army. Its responsibilities include development, procurement, storage, delivery, and maintenance. It is headquartered at Redstone Arsenal, Ala.

The United States Army Network Enterprise Technology Command (NETCOM) is a DRU responsible for the Army's worldwide communications system, including air traffic control facilities. It is headquartered at Fort Huachuca, Ariz.

The United States Army Medical Command (MEDCOM) is a DRU that provides health services for Army personnel and supervises medical training and education. It is headquartered at Fort Sam Houston, Tex.

The United States Army Intelligence and Security Command (INSCOM) performs intelligence and security functions above the corps level. It is headquartered at Fort Belvoir, Va.

The Military Surface Deployment and Distribution Command is an ASCC that controls the movement of freight, personal property, and passengers for the Department of Defense. Another duty is the administration of highways for national defense. It is headquartered at Scott Air Force Base, Ill.

The United States Army Military District of Washington (MDW), which supports the activities of the Army and of the Department of Defense, is the DRU primarily responsible for protecting the nation's capital. Other duties include arranging state funerals and supervising military participation in ceremonies for foreign dignitaries. It is headquartered at Fort McNair in Washington, D.C.

The United States Army Criminal Investigation Command (USACIDC) is responsible for all criminal investigations that are conducted by the Army, including those overseas. It operates a criminal intelligence element. It is headquartered at Quantico, Va.

The United States Army Corps of Engineers is a DRU responsible for both military engineering projects and civil works programs. It is headquartered at Washington, D.C.

A member of the United States Army Corps of Engineers inspects a U.S.-funded water treatment plant in Fallujah, Iraq. Scott Peterson/ Getty Images

The United States Army Test and Evaluation Command (ATEC) is a DRU responsible for testing and evaluation of military systems. It is headquartered at Aberdeen Proving Ground, Md.

The United States Army Acquisition Support Center (USAASC) is a DRU that oversees the conceptualization, development, and acquisition of military systems. It is headquartered at Fort Belvoir, Va.

The United States Army Installation Management Command maintains services and facilities for Army personnel and their families. It is headquartered at Fort Sam Houston, Tex.

In addition to these commands, there are six Army regional Component Commands. The United States Army Africa (USARAF) is headquartered in Vicenza, Italy. The United States Army Europe (USAREUR) is headquartered in Weisbaden, Germany. The United States Army Central (Third Army/ARCENT) oversees central Asia and the Middle East and it is headquartered at Shaw Air Force Base, S.C. The United States Army North (Fifth Army/ARNORTH) and United States Army South (ARSOUTH) oversee North and South America, respectively and both are headquartered at Fort Sam Houston, Tex. The United States Army Pacific (USARPAC) oversees the Pacific region and it is headquartered at Fort Shafter, Hawaii. Other DRUs include the United States Army Reserve Command (USARC) and the United States Military Academy at West Point. Additional ASCCs include the United States Army Special Operations Command (USASOC) and the United States Army Space and Missile Defense

Command/Army Strategic Command (USASMDC/ARSTRAT).

ARMS AND DIVISIONS

The branches of the Army fall into three broad categories: combat arms, combat support arms, and sustainment arms. Combinations of these arms function as teams.

Combat arms are the branches that are directly involved in fighting. They include the infantry, armor, air defense artillery, field artillery, and aviation.

The infantry engages the enemy by using firepower and maneuvers. Although infantrymen may be transported by any means, they normally fight on foot. The infantry is the basic fighting force, but it functions as a part of a team that includes other arms.

Armor conducts mounted mobile, land, and air cavalry warfare. Most armor units are organized around a nucleus of tanks.

Air defense artillery destroys enemy aircraft and missiles. It is also capable of attacking ground targets with guns, missiles, and automatic weapons.

Field artillery also destroys enemy targets and is the primary support for infantry and armor. Its weapons include both cannon and missiles.

Aviation primarily works with field troops. A group of aircraft assigned to a field unit is under the control of the commander of the unit.

Combat support arms are branches of the Army including the Corps of Engineers, the Signal Corps, the Military Police Corps, the Chemical Corps, and Military Intelligence.

—The Corps of Engineers has combat units that are responsible for construction and demolition.

—The Signal Corps installs, operates, and maintains communications and electronic equipment.

—The Military Police Corps performs such duties as supervising prisoners of war, preventing crime, and providing security.

—The Chemical Corps assists combat units principally through activities such as reconnaissance and decontamination of chemical, biological, or nuclear threats.

—Military Intelligence units provide background information on the enemy and on the weather and terrain. They also monitor enemy communications and interrogate prisoners of war.

Sustainment arms are branches of the Army that perform logistics and administrative functions that support the combat arms. Sustainment arms include: Adjutant General's Corps; Corps of Engineers; Finance Corps; Ordnance Corps; Quartermaster Corps; Judge Advocate General's Corps; Transportation Corps; Chaplains; and the six branches of the Army Medical Department—Army Medical Specialist Corps, Army Nurse Corps, Dental Corps, Medical Corps, Medical Service Corps, and Veterinary Corps.

THE DIVISION

The division is the smallest force that includes all of the combat arms and support arms of the Army. The standard elements of a division are a headquarters and headquarters company; an aviation battalion; an air defense artillery battalion; an engineer battalion; a combat electronic warfare and intelligence battalion; an armored cavalry squadron; a signal battalion; a chemical company; a military police company; a division field artillery headquarters with attached field artillery firing battalions; a support command that provides medical, transportation, supply, field maintenance, and administrative services; and three or more combat brigades.

Several divisions make up a corps. Two or more corps comprise a field army. Two or more field armies make up a group.

The infantry division uses the foot soldier as its basic component. It is the oldest type of division and continues to be the core of the Army.

The armored division uses the tank as its principal weapon. This type of division developed after World War I.

The airborne division uses Air Force and Army aircraft to drop troops by parachute behind enemy lines or in remote places. After they land, paratroopers fight as infantrymen.

The mechanized infantry division relies on several types of combat vehicles. This type of division was first organized in the mid-1960s.

The airmobile division uses helicopters for transport and for fire support. This type of division was also developed during the mid-1960s.

SPECIAL FORCES

The Special Forces of the Army are trained to infiltrate deep behind an enemy's lines

Soldiers representing five of the seven Special Forces groups stand in their signature green berets in Arlington National Cemetery in Virginia. Only members of the Special Forces may wear the green beret. DVIDS/Sgt. 1st Class Gonzalo (John) Gonzalez

and to carry on guerrilla warfare. Because of the hazards of this type of fighting the Special Forces is made up entirely of volunteers. Special Forces candidates first complete basic and advanced training and the basic airborne course. They are then assigned to the Special Forces Training Group, located at Fort Bragg, N.C. Upon

DELTA FORCE

The Army's 1st Special Forces Operational Detachment-Delta, better known as Delta Force, is a unit primarily tasked with irregular warfare and counterterrorism. Crafted in the mold of Britain's Special Air Service, Delta Force was created by U.S. Army Col. Charles Beckwith in 1977 as a military response to terrorist threats that had emerged in the 1970s. The unit had an inauspicious start, when one of its earliest missions, the attempted rescue of American hostages in Iran, ended in disaster. Later missions were far less conspicuous, and it is believed that Delta operators were active in the wars in Iraq and Afghanistan. While much about the unit remains secret, the selection process is said to be extremely rigorous, testing the physical, mental, and psychological fitness of each prospective recruit. Successful candidates join one of three operational squadrons (A, B, or C), with further subdivisions based on individual skills and mission requirements.

completion of training they become members of 12-man detachments, the basic Special Forces unit.

A Special Forces detachment is made up of two officers and ten noncommissioned officers. Each of the noncommissioned officers is proficient in one of the five basic Special Forces skills. Two are skilled in the use of all types of weapons. Another two are communications experts. A third pair, trained in medicine, are capable of performing limited surgery and of treating illnesses and diseases common to a particular region. A fourth pair are demolitions specialists. The fifth pair are senior noncommissioned officers trained in operations and intelligence.

All members of a Special Forces detachment also have training in the areas outside their specialties. Many are proficient in a foreign language or receive language training after assignment.

U.S. Central Command

U.S. Central Command (CENTCOM) is a regional unified command of the United States military. Established in 1983 in response to the Iran-Iraq War and the Soviet campaign in Afghanistan, CENTCOM has an area of responsibility that covers central Asia and the Middle East. For this reason, it has played a key role in the ongoing U.S.-led campaign against terrorist groups based in that region, and it combats piracy in the Arabian Sea in concert with U.S. Africa Command (AFRICOM). It is headquartered at MacDill Air Force Base, Florida.

CHAPTER 8

HISTORY OF THE UNITED STATES ARMY

After the American Revolution the Continental Congress declared its belief that a standing army was contrary to democratic principles, and it disbanded the veteran forces. It soon found, however, that regular troops were needed to protect the frontier forts and lands against Indians and other enemies of settlers. When the government was organized under the Constitution, there was a force of about 1,000 officers and enlisted men.

THE AMERICAN ARMY IN THE 19TH CENTURY

The country entered the War of 1812 with only about 7,000 trained soldiers. After the war Congress authorized a regular force of 10,000. At the outbreak of war with Mexico in 1846 the Regular Army consisted of only about 8,000. This small force, augmented by volunteers, won the Mexican War. Congress then authorized strengthening the Army

Minutemen—members of the colonial militia during the American Revolution—gather together and prepare to fight. Militias aided the Continental Army during the Revolutionary War. **MPI/Archive Photos/ Getty Images**

to 18,000 men. This force furnished the framework for the Northern armies of the Civil War.

After the Civil War Congress set the size of the Regular Army at 45,000 men but later reduced it to 25,000. Most of these men saw constant service in the Indian wars in the West. The Army was primarily an Indian-fighting force when war erupted with Spain in 1898, but Spain's weakness and the success of the Navy soon ended the conflict. After the war the United States had to garrison overseas possessions, necessitating an increase in Army strength to 100,000 men.

THE AMERICAN ARMY DURING THE WORLD WARS

The National Defense Act of 1916 created the framework of the Army that fought in World War I. The act increased the strength of the Regular Army to 287,846 men and provided for a reserve corps of officers and enlisted men. It also authorized the president to call the state National Guard units into federal service. Most of the American forces in World War I, however, were raised by means of the Selective Service Act of 1917. Of the 3,700,000 men under arms at the end of the war, 2,800,000 had been drafted into the service.

In the years of peace that followed, lack of Congressional appropriations cut the Army's strength to 12,000 officers and 118,000 enlisted men. In 1939 President Franklin D. Roosevelt's proclamation of a "limited emergency" included an order to increase the size of the Regular Army and the National Guard. The first National Guards and Reserves were called into federal service in 1940.

Swift expansion of the Army resulted from the Selective Training and Service Act of 1940. The United States entered World War II with a force of 1,600,000 men. By 1945 the Army had 8,300,000 men. Two-thirds of them were drafted through Selective Service. With this force the Army organized 89 combat divisions. These consisted of 66 infantry, 16 armored, five airborne, one dismounted cavalry, and one mountain division.

After V-J Day (victory over Japan in August 1945) the Army demobilized rapidly. By 1947 the number of men on active duty had fallen below the authorized peacetime strength of 670,000. National Guard and Organized Reserve enlistments, however, were greater than ever. The Selective Service Act of 1948 established a peacetime draft. In 1947 the Army Air Force was separated from the Army. It became the United States Air Force, coequal with the Army and the Navy. In addition, control of some operations was withdrawn from the individual services and placed under the Joint Chiefs of Staff.

THE KOREAN AND VIETNAM WARS

At the outbreak of the Korean War in 1950 the draft was extended to 1959. (It was extended for additional four-year periods in 1959, in 1963, and in 1967, and was extended for a two-year period in 1971.) During the Korean War the Army expanded to more than 20 combat divisions.

The Reserve Forces Act of 1955 initiated compulsory reserve training. It enabled men from 17 to 18 1/2 years of age to enlist in the Ready or the Standby Reserve. In 1963 the reorganization of National Guard and Organized Reserve divisions under the ROAD plan was completed. The period of service for reservists was cut from eight to six years. Further restructuring of the Army Reserve and Army National Guard was ordered in 1965.

Beginning in the mid-1950s, United States Army personnel served in South Vietnam in an advisory capacity. After United States bases were attacked by the Viet Cong in 1965, the Army played an active part in the Vietnam War. By 1968 seven Army divisions, plus other units, were fighting in Vietnam.

General Douglas MacArthur speaks with U.S. soldiers in South Korea at the beginning of the Korean War. Carl Mydans/Time & Life Pictures/ Getty Images

Army manpower totaled about 1,470,000. After the war manpower was about 830,000.

During the 1960s many people criticized Selective Service. Some critics opposed United States military involvement in Vietnam. Many argued, however, that the system itself was unfair since, through its exemptions, it allowed certain groups— for example, college students—to escape military service. To correct such inequities, Congress instituted a draft lottery in 1969.

In January 1973, six months before the Selective Service Act expired, the draft was ended, and the Army began using all-volunteer forces. The Army, and the other armed services, attracted disproportionate numbers of blacks and of poor, undereducated volunteers. In addition, low pay scales caused reenlistment rates to drop. Registration, without conscription, was resumed in 1980. In the early 1990s the United States Army had a strength of 731,700, with reserves of almost the same number in the Army National Guard and the Army Reserves combined. Units of the Army were deployed in the continental United States, Alaska, Hawaii, Europe, Asia, and Latin America.

THE PERSIAN GULF WAR

During the Persian Gulf War in early 1991 the Allied coalition against Iraq reached a strength of more than 700,000 troops, including 539,000 American personnel. After a massive Allied air war lasting several weeks the Allies sent in large numbers of ground troops to destroy Iraqi fortifications, weapons stockpiles, and tanks. Within four days the Allies had destroyed most of Iraq's elite Republican Guard and Pres. George H.W. Bush had declared a cease-fire. After the war, proposals were made by Congress to cut the total armed forces by some 22 percent over the next five years.

DON'T ASK, DON'T TELL

The term "Don't Ask, Don't Tell" was coined after Pres. Bill Clinton in 1993 signed a law directing that military personnel "don't ask, don't tell, don't pursue, and don't harass" on matters of homosexuals serving in the U.S. military. When it went into effect on

Oct. 1, 1993, the policy theoretically lifted a ban on homosexual service that had been instituted during World War II, though in effect it continued a statutory ban. Under the terms of the law, homosexuals serving in the military were not allowed to talk about their sexual orientation or engage in sexual activity, and commanding officers were not allowed to question service members about their sexual orientation. For a variety of reasons, the policy did little to change the behavior of commanders; gay and lesbian soldiers continued to be discharged from service. By the 15-year anniversary of the law

Activists supporting the repeal of the "Don't Ask, Don't Tell" policy rallying on Capitol Hill in Washington, D.C. Alex Wong/Getty Images

in 2008, more than 12,000 officers had been discharged from the military for refusing to hide their homosexuality. When Barack Obama campaigned for the presidency in 2008, he pledged to overturn "Don't Ask, Don't Tell" and to allow gay men and lesbians to serve openly in the military. In December 2010 both the House of Representatives and the Senate voted to repeal the policy, and President Obama signed the legislation on December 22. The policy officially ended on September 20, 2011.

THE AFGHANISTAN WAR

The September 11, 2001, attacks on the United States were a spectacular example of the asymmetrical warfare that conventional 20th-century armies were ill equipped to combat. As a result, the CIA initially took the lead in Afghanistan, using local tribesmen as a force multiplier to overturn the Taliban regime that had hosted al-Qaeda. As the focus of the administration of Pres. George W. Bush shifted to Iraq in 2003, Afghanistan was treated in some ways as "the forgotten war." The Taliban used this reprieve to regroup and rebuild its strength, while the remaining U.S. troops assisted with nation-building efforts. As the war in Iraq wound down in 2009, lessons learned by insurgents there were exported to Afghanistan, and U.S. casualties jumped sharply. A "surge" of 30,000 additional troops authorized by Pres. Barack Obama in 2009–10 allowed Afghan forces the opportunity to rebuild and ultimately assume some of the security burden.

THE IRAQ WAR

When U.S. troops returned to Iraq in March 2003, they did so in numbers that were a fraction of those deployed in 1991. This "light footprint" strategy relied heavily on the overwhelming technological edge enjoyed by the U.S.-led coalition; this advantage was on full display in the "shock and awe" bombardment that opened the war. Although this demonstration did not lead to the immediate capitulation of Iraqi forces, the U.S. advance on Baghdad was slowed more by the weather than it was by effective and concentrated Iraqi resistance. Pres. George W. Bush declared an end to major combat operations on May 1, 2003, but the war in Iraq was far from over.

U.S. troops who were sent to Iraq following the 2007 surge keep low after hearing gunshots while on patrol. **David Furst/AFP/Getty Images**

With Iraq's ruling Ba'th Party purged from the government and security forces, no domestic force was capable of enforcing order, and criminality and sectarian violence spiraled out of control. U.S. forces, unable to find the weapons of mass destruction that served as the war's rationale, found themselves engaged in a civil war between rival Shī'ite and Sunni militias. As the U.S. death toll climbed, recruitment numbers dropped,

WOMEN IN COMBAT

Beginning in World War II, women began to occupy an increasingly conspicuous role in the United States Army. More than 150,000 women served in the Women's Army Auxiliary Corps (later the Women's Army Corps, or WAC), working as nurses, mechanics, clerks, and intelligence analysts. In the massive demobilization that followed the war, most of these women returned to civilian life, but the success of the WAC led to its integration into the regular Army. The WAC existed as a separate corps within the Army until 1978, when it was abolished and women were integrated into all aspects of Army life except combat duty. That distinction became increasingly suspect given the nature of asymmetrical warfare in the 21st century. No longer could personnel serving in traditional noncombat roles be considered outside the theater of combat, as there were no fixed front lines. As a result, more than 130 female troops from various branches of service were killed in the wars in Iraq and Afghanistan. Faced with this reality, in January 2013 the Department of Defense lifted the ban on women in combat. As combat experience is a significant consideration for promotion at virtually all ranks, the change was seen as a boost to the advancement prospects for women throughout the Army.

and the Army was forced to adopt alternative methods to bolster its thinning ranks. National Guard units were deployed to Iraq, and thousands of reservists were called up to active duty. A controversial measure, known as stop-loss, prevented troops scheduled for deployment from leaving the military. Tens of thousands of active-duty soldiers and reservists were affected by the policy, which was criticized by some as a "back door draft." As the security situation in Iraq became more tenuous and criticism of the U.S. occupation increased, a "surge" of U.S. troops in early 2007 is thought to have been one possible factor in the declining level of violence.

By the time U.S. troops left Iraq in December 2011, almost 4,500 Americans had been killed and some 30,000 had been wounded, with the Army accounting for the overwhelming majority in both categories. One very concrete change for the Army that was spurred by the wars in Iraq and Afghanistan was the replacement for the venerable M16 rifle. The M4 carbine, a rifle that shared the AR-15 platform with the M16, was adopted as the Army's standard infantry weapon. The M16's ability to accurately shoot at distances of more than 547 yards (500 m) was largely wasted in the short-range engagements that were typical of modern wars. The smaller size of the M4 also made it better suited for the Army's patrol doctrine, which involved frequently mounting and dismounting from vehicles.

CONCLUSION

As security needs and the demands of war evolved over the millennia, so too did armies around the world. In addition to adopting new technology and weaponry throughout the centuries, armies have also changed in composition and structure. While most countries today have a national standing army, this was not always the case; few ancient civilizations had organized armies, and many countries that later did often augmented their numbers with mercenary forces. Present-day armies have a set command structure and are comprised of individuals—in many cases both men and women—from all walks of life.

From ancient times to the present day, soldiers have demonstrated courage, honor, and sacrifice, many laying down their lives in the line of duty. Although modern armies in many ways differ greatly from those that came before, they remain as vital to the countries and causes for which they fight.

GLOSSARY

asymmetrical warfare Warfare between opposing forces differing greatly in military power that typically involves the use of unconventional weapons and tactics (such as those associated with guerrilla warfare and terrorist attacks).

blitzkrieg War conducted with great speed and force; specifically a violent surprise offensive by massed air forces and mechanized ground forces in close coordination.

caliphate The political-religious state comprising the Muslim community and the lands and peoples under its dominion in the centuries following the death of the Prophet Muhammad.

cavalry The component of an army mounted on horseback or moving in motor vehicles and having combat missions (as reconnaissance and counterreconnaissance) that require great mobility.

centurion An officer of the ancient Roman army who commanded one hundred men.

commando A military unit, or member of such a unit, trained and organized as shock troops especially for hit-and-run raids into enemy territory.

conscription Compulsory enrollment of persons especially for military service.

containment The policy or the process of preventing the expansion beyond prescribed limits of a hostile power, ideology, or inimical forces especially by employing political, economic, and propaganda pressure and by strengthening friendly powers.

drone An unmanned aircraft or ship guided by remote control.

garrison To supply (a military post) with troops for defense.

hoplite A heavily armed infantry soldier of ancient Greece.

infantry Soldiers trained, armed, and equipped to fight on foot.

insurgent A person who rises in revolt against civil authority or an established government; rebel, especially a rebel not recognized as a belligerent.

legion The principal unit of the Roman army comprising at first 3,000 but later 5,000 to 6,000 foot soldiers with a complement of cavalry.

man-at-arms A heavily armed and usually mounted soldier.

maniple A subdivision of the Roman legion consisting of either 120 or 60 men.

mercenary A soldier hired into foreign service.

military-industrial complex An informal alliance of the military and related government departments with defense industries that is held to influence government policy.

phalanx In military science, tactical formation consisting of a block of heavily armed infantry standing shoulder to shoulder in files several ranks deep.

sectarian Confined to the limits of one religious group, one school, or one party.

selective service A system under which men are called up for military service.

standing army A permanent army of paid soldiers.

stop-loss In the U.S. military, a policy that extends a service member's tour beyond the date his or her term of service is scheduled to end.

strafe To rake (as ground troops) with fire at close range and especially with machine-gun fire from low-flying aircraft.

FOR MORE INFORMATION

The Army Historical Foundation
2425 Wilson Boulevard
Arlington, VA 22201
(800) 506-2672
Web site: https://armyhistory.org
The Army Historical Foundation is a non-
profit organization dedicated to preserving the stories and artifacts of the United
States Army, restoring important historical buildings and landmarks related to
the Army, and supporting the National
Museum of the United States Army.

Canadian War Museum
1 Vimy Place
Ottawa, ON K1A 0M8
Canada
(800) 555-5621
Web site: http://www.warmuseum.ca
Through exhibitions featuring art, arti-
facts, and memoirs, as well as interactive

presentations, the Canadian War Museum engages visitors with the history of the Canadian military from its inception to the present. It also offers a variety of educational programs on the history of the Canadian armed forces.

Directorate of History and Heritage (DHH)
National Defence Headquarters
101 Colonel By Drive
Ottawa, ON K1A 0K2
Canada
(613) 998-7058
Web site: http://www.cmp-cpm.forces.gc.ca/ dhh-dhp/index-eng.asp
The DHH is an organization under the Canadian Department of National Defence dating back to the First World War. Its museum system and publications offer a wealth of information on the history of the Canadian Forces for researchers and the general public.

The Society of Ancient Military Historians (SAMH)
History Department, Western Illinois University
Morgan Hall 445
Macomb, IL 61455-1390
(309) 298-1053

Web site: http://ccat.sas.upenn.edu/rrice/
samh.html
The SAMH publishes the *Res Militares*
newsletter featuring articles and research
on the study of warfare in the ancient
world. The society meets with members
as well as the academic community to
share research and topics of special inter-
est regarding warfare in antiquity.

U.S Army Center of Military History
102 4th Avenue, Building 35
Fort McNair, DC 20319
(202) 685-2733
Web site: http://www.history.army.mil
The U.S. Army Center of Military History
is a directorate within the office of the
administrative assistant to the Secretary
of the Army. It provides books, research
materials, and information on the history
of the United States Army, its organizational structure, and its units.

U.S. Army Heritage and Education Center
(USAHEC)
950 Soldiers Drive
Carlisle, PA 17013
(717) 245-3972

Web site: http://usahec.org

The USAHEC is the leading museum and research facility of the United States Army, dedicated to preserving the legacy of soldiers of the Army. Its museum, research facility, and events are free and open to the public.

WEB SITES

Due to the changing nature of Internet links, Rosen Educational Services has developed an online list of Web sites related to the subject of this book. This site is updated regularly. Please use this link to access the list:

http://www.rosenlinks.com/armed/army

FOR FURTHER READING

Behnke, Alison. *The Conquests of Genghis Khan*. Minneapolis, MN: Twenty-First Century, 2008.

Beller, Susan Provost. *The Doughboys Over There: Soldiering in World War I*. Minneapolis, MN: Twenty-First Century, 2007.

Beller, Susan Provost. *Roman Legions on the March: Soldiering in the Ancient Roman Army*. Minneapolis MN: Twenty-First Century, 2007.

Bingham, Jane. *The Gulf Wars with Iraq*. Chicago, IL: Heinemann-Raintree, 2012.

Dolan, Edward F. *Careers in the U.S. Army*. New York, NY: Benchmark, 2009.

Earl, C.F., and Gabrielle Vanderhoof. *Army Rangers*. Broomall, PA: Mason Crest, 2010.

Gillard, Arthur. *The War in Afghanistan*. San Diego, CA: Greenhaven, 2013.

Immell, Myra. *The Korean War*. San Diego, CA: Greenhaven, 2011.

Lai, Benjamin. *The Chinese People's Liberation Army Since 1949: Ground Forces*. Oxford, England: Osprey, 2012.

Porterfield, Jason. *Your Career in the Army*. New York, NY: Rosen Publishing Group, 2011.

Rogers, H.C.B. *Napoleon's Army*. Barnsley, England: Pen & Sword, 2005.

INDEX